g. b. taylor
184

ARCHITECTURAL DRAWING:
THE ART AND THE PROCESS

ARCHITECTURAL DRAWING: THE ART AND THE PROCESS

by Gerald Allen and Richard Oliver

WHITNEY LIBRARY OF DESIGN
an imprint of Watson-Guptill Publications/New York

The Architectural Press Ltd./London

First published 1981 in the United States and Canada by Whitney Library of Design,
an imprint of Watson-Guptill Publications,
a division of Billboard Publications, Inc.,
1515 Broadway, New York, N.Y.10036

Library of Congress Cataloging in Publication Data
Main entry under title:
Architectural drawing.
   1. Architectural drawing—United States. I. Allen,
Gerald. II. Oliver, Richard, 1942–
NA2706.U6A7   720'.28'4   81-10339
ISBN 0-8230-7043-3   AACR2

Published in Great Britain by The Architectural Press Ltd.,
9 Queen Anne's Gate, London SW1H 9BY
ISBN 0 85139 734 4

Manufactured in U.S.A.

First Printing, 1981

CONTENTS

ACKNOWLEDGMENTS

The authors would like to thank Sharon Lee Ryder of the Whitney Library of Design, who first proposed the idea of this book. We also wish to thank Stephen Kliment who took up the project in midstream and oversaw its completion with great sensitivity. In addition we appreciate the patience, enthusiasm, and thoroughness with which Susan Davis guided the project through all the intricacies of the production process.

We are also grateful and therefore would like to offer our thanks to the Henry L. Meltzer Group, Inc., for access to the electronic word processor on which the text was written and edited.

PREFACE

The collection of new American architectural drawings in this book is based in part on an exhibition, "Creation and Recreation: America Draws," which was organized and shown by the Museum of Finnish Architecture in Helsinki and which has subsequently been exhibited in other major cities in Western Europe. The American participants were naturally flattered that a country like Finland with an old and distinguished tradition of fine architecture would be so actively interested in the contemporary architecture of America, and they are grateful to the director of the museum, other members of the museum staff, and other Finnish architects and institutions for the friendly assistance provided in Helsinki on the American's behalf. They are also grateful to the Consulate of Finland in New York and to the Cultural Counsellor of Finland for expediting the transportation of the original drawings abroad.

In appreciation for all of these efforts on the part of the Finnish people, the authors dedicate this volume to the Museum of Finnish Architecture.

PART 1

THE ART, THE PROCESS, AND THE MEANING

It is a pleasure for the authors of this book to be able to introduce its contents to a broad general audience as well as to our professional colleagues. We can do this because architecture has lately become a fashionable topic, and architects veritable media phenomena. Their work is widely discussed, featured in newspapers and magazines, and exhibited in museums. Doubtless all this has much to do with the growing sense of concern evoked in nearly all of us by the state of the physical world we find ourselves inhabiting. It also has to do, we hope, with the chance that our world may still be improved and that good architecture will somehow help.

One striking event in the emerging popularity of our subject is not just the new interest in architecture, but the remarkable reemergence of interest in architectural drawings. It had become almost traditional over the past half century for architects to make skillful but still somewhat matter-of-fact drawings to aid in the construction of a building or to portray its physical features to clients or to the architectural press. Now, however, extraordinarily beautiful drawings are being made to illustrate buildings, as before, but also more explicitly the ideas that shaped them, and even polemical theories about architecture itself. These are now bought by collectors for whom they are works of art as well as talismans of architecture.

It is arguable that the best ideas in architecture today are being found more on paper, and on plastic and photographic film and the other new mediums now being used, than in actual buildings. Whether or not this is fully true, the mere presence of drawings on the current architectural scene after their long absence is without a doubt a singular feature of late-twentieth-century design, particularly as it is practiced in the United States. If one is interested in what is going on in American architecture, then one must look at, among other things, architectural drawings. They are messengers bearing tidings of new events and ideas in this now popular art, and they are also carrying implicit signs of mistrust and disappointment with the architecture of the recent past and with the world it has helped to produce.

Notable, nonetheless, is the very multiplicity of messages that drawings are now delivering. The collection of them shown in this book, which comes from architects in many different parts of the country and from established as well as younger ones still at the beginnings of their careers, fully documents this variety. So it will not be surprising if the reader, faced with our collage, becomes somewhat perplexed and immediately asks what on earth is going on. Drawings are manifestations of what architecture is about and what its specific relationships to social purposes

1. Mirador in the cloister of the
Church of San Estevan, Acoma, New Mexico,
about 1644. (Photograph: Gerald Allen)

can be. These relationships are strong, as we shall see. So the initial perplexed question of what is going on in American architectural drawings will beckon us further along a pathway that leads to a greater perplex still: what is going on today in America itself, in its culture, its society, its politics, its economy, and its ethics? All these larger issues will be addressed in the process of introducing the drawings that follow.

First, though, it is worth raising a still more obvious pair of issues: what is an architectural drawing, and what is its relationship to architecture itself?

PRIMARY
REPRESENTATION

Architecture, sculpture, and painting may be regarded as material arts, because in all of them an artistic intention is forged into physical matter at one moment in time; a building is built, a piece of sculpture is sculpted, and a painting is painted. After that, the artifact that has resulted remains unchanged, save for the ravages of physical decay, accident, or human malevolence. In these same terms, we might also describe literature, music, dance, and drama as nonmaterial arts, because their intentions are woven mainly into a set of directions. These in turn are rendered into an artistic event again and again throughout the course of time; the music is played, the poem is chanted or read, the dance and the play performed.

It is important for us to realize that what we are calling material and nonmaterial arts each have their own very distinct meanings for us and that these are quite different from their particular content and are in fact transmitted implicitly through their mediums. This is a peculiar fact that is often not recognized by even sophisticated observers of art. Objects of material art, for instance, stand like monuments—palpable affirmations of humanity's ancient longing for a continuity of things and for an endurance of human endeavor. Consider the case of a venerable assembly of nothing but mud and stone and wood like the seventeenth-century church of San Estevan at Acoma in New Mexico (1). It has meaning not just for the pious and also the political intentions it embodies; these are among the things that would conventionally be regarded as its content. But surely as well it has meaning simply as a thing. It has meaning because it has merely existed as a physical object since human intentions were first laboriously embodied in it and because it still does exist centuries later as we stand and look at it. So too with sculptures and paintings. As they stand or hang in their places they have as artifacts meanings that again are independent of their specific contents: they are silent physical objects, made by people, existing in time, and affirming the human dream of continuity and endurance.

Nonmaterial art, however, makes an opposite affirmation through its mediums. It is a witness to the miracle of the human imagination and to the phenomenon of human creativity. But by being this it also brings with it, by definition, the certainty of change and with that the concurrent fact of decay. The spirit of a poem can spring to life over and over again, just as the experience of it quickly fades. A string quartet tantalizes not just for its interlacing progressions of harmonies and patterns of rhythms that finally result in a completed sonic whole, but also because the whole never exists at once and its parts immediately pass away. And such is the case in the dance and also in the drama; both are artifices that do not endure, and either consciously or unconsciously we are all aware of that. In their particular realizations in time, they are unique, ceremonial, and ephemeral, and this is surely as critical a part of their meaning as what we recognize as their content.

SECONDARY REPRESENTATIONS

All the arts just described—of physical form and of language, sound, and gesture—are primary representations. Secondary representations are of two obvious types: those that come before the work of art and predict what it may be like and those that come afterward and describe what it is or was. The first category includes notes, studies, drafts, maquettes, models, sketches, and drawings. The second includes recordings, photographs and other mechanical reproductions, and, again, sketches and drawings. The function of both kinds of secondary representations of art is to make accessible to secondary audiences what the primary representation could become, what it may actually be, or what it perhaps was.

Architecture is, quite obviously, a three-dimensional, material art. Much less obvious, however, is the fact that the experience of architecture is not simply visual. The rich store of mental images, for instance, possessed by all of us and held in memory is not only useful but indeed critical to informing the three-dimensional reality of architecture with meaning. But also crucial, and possibly more difficult to understand, are those perceptual dimensions in addition to the visual one that are technically known as *haptic*: the bodily senses other than sight, smell, taste, and hearing. The haptic dimensions include an expanded sense of touch that incorporates the entire body and influences our perceptions of things. These haptic perceptions include our sense of the size of a building relative to our own size, for example, and the senses of being near to it or far from it,

2. The Washington Monument seen from the West Front of the United States Capitol, Washington, D.C., 1848–1885. (Photograph: Paul David Birnbaum)

enclosed or unenclosed, over or under, up or down, left or right, and before or behind.

The existance of these haptic perceptions, and their importance, can explain why even so clear and simple a construction as, for instance, the Washington Monument (2) is best appreciated by actually being there. Presumably that is exactly why so many people do not just stay at home and look at it in photographs, but instead go there annually in prodigious numbers to see it from afar, look at it up close from various sides, climb up the inside, and peer out from the top.

The full experience of architecture comes from appreciating these kinds of things, which can only be perceived from architecture's primary representation. The full experience of architecture, in other words, emerges from all our perceptual responses to the actual thing—the things we see, the things our minds remind us we have seen previously, and the things we experience through our haptic senses. This fact, in turn, explains precisely why—in spite of many claims to the contrary in this heyday of the architectural drawing—drawings are not architecture. It also explains why it is simply impossible for drawings to evoke the perceptions that architecture evokes, no matter how vividly they may suggest them.

To point all this out is not by any means to slight the importance of architectural drawings, only to place that importance properly. In architecture, the drawing through history has often played, as it does now, the role of prophet, predicting what architecture might be long before the structures of society, politics, and economics are prepared to receive it. The world of architecture, now as then, would be the poorer if that performance were missing, since surely there is a necessary and urgent place in our world for the prophetic, just as there is also an equally legitimate place for convention. Recent advocates of so-called paper architecture, however, have in their understandable zeal sometimes distorted the time-honored relationship between drawing and architecture and between delineator and architect. Architectural drawings are secondary, not primary, representations of art.

ARCHITECTURAL DRAWINGS AS SECONDARY REPRESENTATIONS

Architectural drawings come both before the work of art in order to predict what it may be like and also after it to describe what it is or was. Thus they are relevant to the entire cycle of design, construction, and evaluation of a building. An architect begins a design by making a variety of sketches and diagrams for what it might be, and almost always these either consciously or unconsciously reflect other buildings and places previously

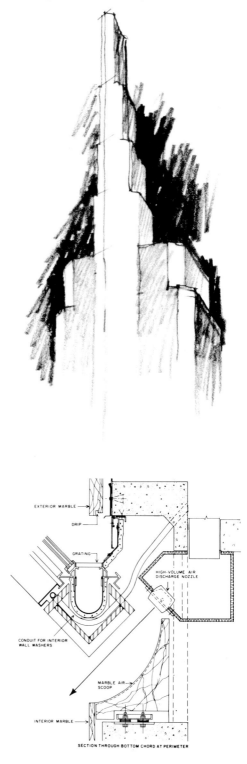

seen and remembered, tempered now by the demands of the particular kind of building that is being requested. In due course, more or less one alternative is settled on; the design is then studied further first in more sketches and then later in refined drawings, as well as in three-dimensional models. Subsequently, the emerging building's physical characteristics are documented in great detail for purposes of construction; these are the working drawings. Then the architect—and often here too his or her staff—draws the built or unbuilt result with the intention of its being published somewhere in a journal or a book—or today, as we are seeing, in the hope of its fetching a high price in a gallery. By doing all these things, the architect hopes to make a small addition to the built world, an embellishment which among other things is then seen by other architects, so that the whole cycle of design, construction, and evaluation can begin anew. A variation of the cycle, which involves what we have called the prophetic, occurs when the designs are intended not for actual construction but to influence and enlighten other architects and interested amateurs. In this case, the working-drawing and construction phases are omitted, and the cycle jumps from the developed design straight to the final presentation drawings.

In an architectural drawing, the rich reality of the building being drawn is always fighting a losing battle with the limitations of the drawing itself. There are two possible consequences of that defeat. One is that the drawing ends up a very poor substitute for the actual thing. The other, and this always happens in a good drawing, is that some aspect of the design deemed important for a particular purpose can, by the exclusion of many other aspects, be more vividly rendered, possibly even more vividly than in the actual building. Two quite simple examples will serve to illustrate this point.

An architect's early design sketches (3), tentative and evocative, can often give a remarkably accurate idea of the overall impression the final building is intended to make, and they usually do this without much regard to many of the details. A construction detail (4), however, can show very precisely how a part of a building is to be assembled without giving, except to the trained observer, any but the faintest clue to what that part may end up looking like. In both cases, many aspects of the building have been disregarded so that a selected few may be regarded specially and intensely. So too with every kind of architectural drawing, and indeed with all architectural drawings. Their power is that they limit what is being portrayed and therefore dramatize certain architectural aspects while muting or even altogether silencing others.

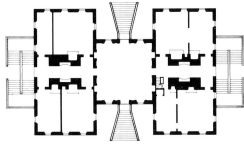

The types of architectural drawings are few. They are merely plan, section, elevation, axonometric, and perspective, plus the combination of these. It is important to realize that all these conventions, with the possible exception of the perspective, represent things that cannot actually be seen.

Plans are imaginary slices taken horizontally through a building, therefore revealing its arrangement of solids and voids. Sections are slices usually taken vertically through a building in order to reveal the same thing, and thus in the strictest sense a section is in fact similar to a plan. What both plans and sections do is draw to our attention spatial relationships that, in fact, can be seen only in the mind's eye. But, nevertheless, they still reveal things that are important to our understanding of a building when we are actually in it. Take first the plan: at least three aspects of the arrangement of a great American house like Stratford Hall in Virginia (5,6,7) would be hard to forget no matter where one happened to be in or around it. They are its overall shape, which is like the letter "H," its formal hall at the center, and its two axes that link this hall to the rest of the house and also to the whole landscape beyond, including formal gardens, fields, and the Potomac River. All three of these things are vividly portrayed in a plan. Now take the section: the most important spatial aspects of a building like the Nebraska State Capitol (8,9) would be equally hard to forget. They are the great height and central position of the tower relative to the rotunda at its base, to other major spaces, and to the low, peripheral building forms. All these things can be exhibited in a sectional drawing.

In contrast to plans and sections, elevations come reasonably close to depicting what the physical eye can see, though two pairs of illustrations will show the false impressions that even these can give. The first is an elevation and a photograph of Gunston Hall in Virginia (10,11), and the second is of St. Thomas Church in New York City (12,13). Since an elevation is an orthographic projection in which all the features of a vertical surface of a building are projected in horizontal lines forward onto an imaginary vertical plane, the result is an image of the building as it could only be seen, theoretically, from an infinite distance. Since in actuality we view buildings closer up, what we see is naturally different and is approximated by the photographs. Notable is the way closer elements stand forward and begin to reveal parts of their sides. Obvious too in the Georgian building is the somewhat reduced prominence of the roof; this always happens in buildings with pitched roofs when the elevation is compared with a photograph or with the real thing. Most obvious of all, of course, is the fact that we do not always look at buildings straight on.

What is known as an axonometric drawing (14) tries to show the forms

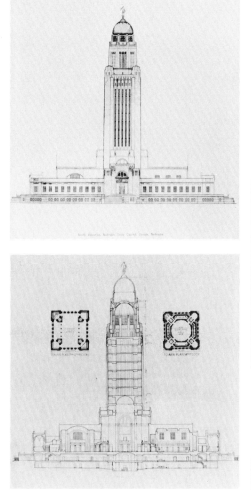

Below:
10. Front elevation of Gunston Hall,
Fairfax County, Virginia,
1758.
(Drawing: Kenneth Clark)

Bottom:
11. Gunston Hall,
Fairfax County, Virginia, 1758.
(Photograph: Gerald Allen)

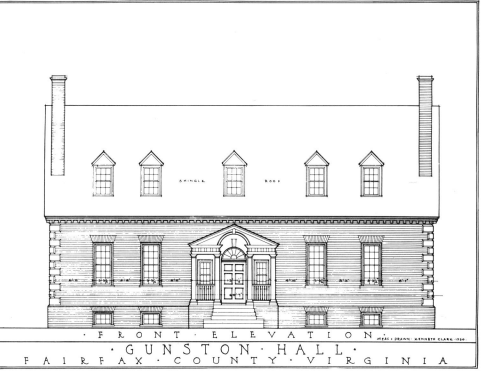

· F R O N T · E L E V A T I O N ·
· G U N S T O N · H A L L ·
F A I R F A X · C O U N T Y · V I R G I N I A

MEAS & DRAWN · KENNETH CLARK · 1930

Top:
8. Front elevation of the Nebraska
State Capitol, Lincoln, 1920–1932.
(Drawing: Bertram Grosvenor
Goodhue Associates)

Above:
9. Section of the Nebraska State
Capitol, Lincoln, 1920–1932.
(Drawing: Bertram Grosvenor
Goodhue Associates)

Above:
12. Saint Thomas Church,
New York City, 1908–1913.
(Photograph: Saint Thomas Church)

Right:
13. Bertram Goodhue's drawing of
the elevation of Saint Thomas Church,
New York City, 1908–1913.

Top to bottom:
15. Isometric drawing of an eight-foot cube.

16. Dimetric drawing of an eight-foot cube.

17. Elevational oblique drawing of an eight-foot cube.

18. Plan oblique drawing of an eight-foot cube.
(Drawings: Richard Oliver)

14. Pringle House,
Charleston, South Carolina, 1744.
(Drawing: William Turnbull)

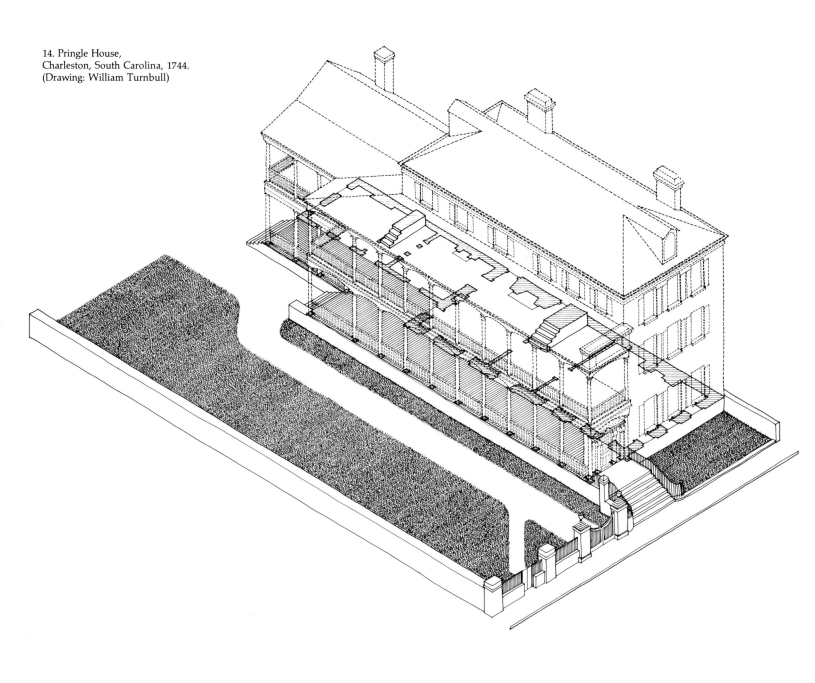

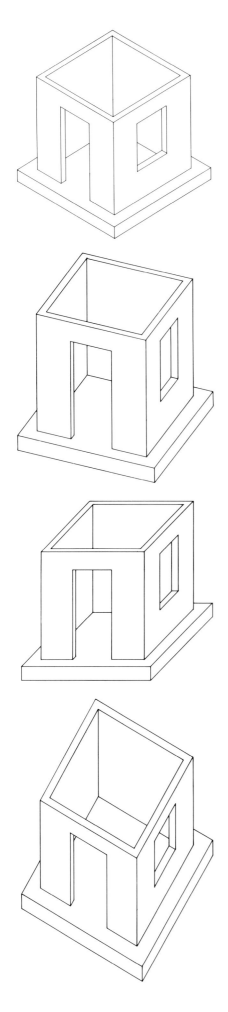

and spaces of a building in something like three true dimensions, but in fact such a drawing is of course distorted—and also incidentally it is imprecisely named. It is a paraline drawing. Such a drawing is distorted because the parallel lines of the actual object are also parallel in the drawing, in contrast to the way an object in space is seen by the eye. There are three types of paraline drawings: isometric, dimetric, and oblique, and each possesses slightly different characteristics. An isometric drawing is the most rigid (15): the three axes and the three visible planes are depicted with equal emphasis. A dimetric drawing is less rigid and more complex (16): the angles between the three axes are variable, measurements can only occur parallel to the three axes, and two measurement scales are required to produce a more realistic representation of an object. In these first two types, no surface is depicted with its true shape, since every plane is distorted in the attempt to suggest a lifelike image of the object from the vantage point of the viewer. The third type is an oblique drawing, and its essential feature is that one surface is depicted with its true shape. In an elevation oblique drawing (17) the vertical planes in one direction are in true shape, and in a plan oblique drawing (18) the true shape of the horizontal surfaces is shown. This last type of drawing is the most popular of all the paraline drawings, and it is also what is commonly known as an axonometric.

All paraline drawings replace the sequential experience of the actual object with an omniscient view of its overall composition. They are impressive, concise, and very easily laid out and drawn. Doubtless for these reasons alone they have recently been one of the most favored drawing types among architects, and for just the same reason they have also become somewhat hackneyed.

One drawing type that does approach actuality—though again like all other drawings it lacks the third spatial dimension as well as the haptic perceptual dimensions—is the perspective. But even in this case there are variations in the degree of fidelity to the actual world, which is suggested by two familiar photographic exercises (19,20). In these illustrations, the same place is photographed using a wide angle and a telescopic lens. This kind of visual distortion, so common in many contemporary photographs, can be approximated in a perspective drawing. This is because any such drawing is a construction of lines connecting points in space. The major elements are the picture plane, the vanishing points on the horizon, the ground line, and the station point that simulates the position in space of the viewer's eye (21). The relationship among these elements can be such that the resulting drawing of an object will be lifelike. But the rela-

19. A building photographed through a 200-mm lens.
(Photograph: Gerald Allen)

20. The same building photographed through a 35-mm lens.
(Photograph: Gerald Allen)

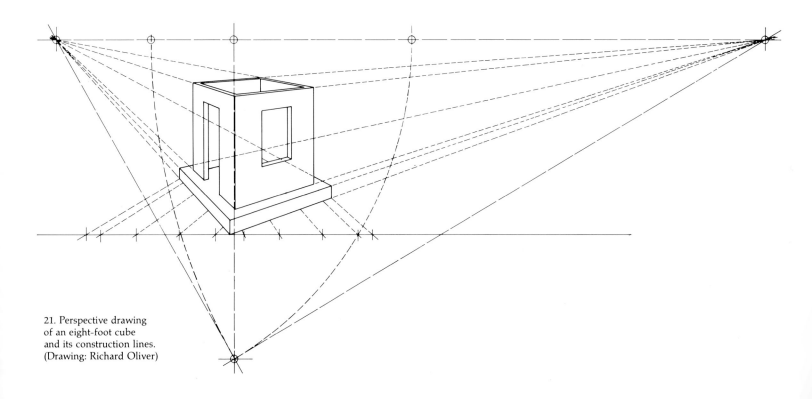

21. Perspective drawing
of an eight-foot cube
and its construction lines.
(Drawing: Richard Oliver)

tionship among these same elements can be rearranged to produce a drawing in which an object may be grossly distorted in apparent size and shape, thus creating a dramatic visual result. Tiny buildings can be rendered to appear bigger, a deep space can be made to appear shallow, and vice versa. These kinds of distortions are relatively easy to manipulate in a perspective, and as a result it has often during the past half century and up until recently been viewed as a somewhat disreputable method of depicting architecture, and it was often supplanted by a three-dimensional model.

The particular kind of drawing an architect makes and its relationship to its audience have varied throughout history. Architects in each generation tend to find their own most useful and favored types. There have been times when the relationship among all the participants in the architectural process—architects, builders, clients, and other users and beholders—was close and when it was more or less clear to all of them what the result was likely to be. This has almost always occurred as the result of a generally understood framework of architectural convention, whether it was Classical, Gothic, some other style that occurred internationally, or indeed a regional vernacular. At such times—which, in general, do not include our own, where a number of conventions exist simultaneously—drawings have assumed relatively less importance than at other times, like ours, when there were greater varieties of precedents and techniques to be considered. As an example of the former case, look, for instance, at a plain and guileless drawing by Thomas Jefferson (22). This is about all that Jefferson drew because this is all he needed to draw for him and other people, mainly the builders, to get the idea. This drawing was for studying the building and for getting it built. By contrast, look at a drawing from the mid-nineteenth-century architect Andrew Jackson Downing, which has a different quality because it is serving a different purpose (23). By Downing's time, the range of choices in America for what a building might be like had expanded considerably, and so Downing's drawings assist the viewer—who was also a prospective buyer—in that choice by depicting an intended result in a scenographic way. Scenographic to the point of being downright lush and seductive is a still later drawing by the early-twentieth-century architect Bertram Goodhue (24). Goodhue's drawing was specifically meant (unsuccessfully, as it turned out) to be so compelling that the client would get swept away and actually build the building.

Today, after the period in American architecture when this kind of drawing was done less and less—a period that generally coincided with the

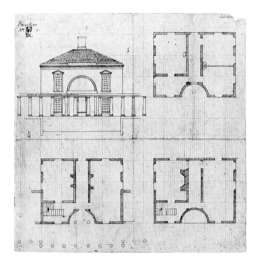

Top:
22. Thomas Jefferson's drawing
of the front elevation and plans
of Pavilion IX at the University
of Virginia, Charlottesville, 1821.

Above:
23. An Italian Villa,
from *The Architecture of Country Houses*
by Andrew Jackson Downing, 1848.

decline of so-called traditional architecture and with the rise of the American phase of the International Style—many architects, including those represented in this collection, are once again exploring the possibilities of varied and enriched communication through the medium of drawing. Some of their drawings are done with dazzling colors and in varying mediums; others are done in cool and precise lines; still others are freely styled and cartoonlike. Some drawings stay well within conventional modes of expression, relying on ink, watercolor and pencil, tracing paper and vellum, while others stretch traditional limits to include collage, bas-relief, photoreproduction, and other new devices. But in each of their different ways, all of them are trying very hard, and in most cases urgently, to tell us something. What is perplexing, as we have already mentioned, is the diversity of signals they are sending out. The collection as a whole is therefore like the proverbial half glass of water. Is the glass half full, or is it half empty? Does the diversity represented here foreshadow a tumble into total confusion, or does it promise a new and rich and multifaceted view of what architecture is and what it can become?

ARCHITECTURAL DRAWINGS AS MEANING

The question still remains of what is the meaning of architectural drawing in America today and therefore what is going on now in American architecture. This can be answered by first asking the question of what, indeed, is going on in America.

At least some clear things are going on. The construction industry annually consumes a smaller and smaller piece of what is unappetizingly known as the Gross National Product, confirming the belief of pessimists that built America in the spectacular sense of yore has indeed been built. Energy, whose apparent inexhaustibility was one of the posits of the International Style, making it possible to build the same kind of building in virtually any climate, has become critically less available, so that to use it other than sparingly is now profligate. In the building business, historic preservation and adaptive reuse have been transformed from a trend in the 1960s and 1970s into a veritable orthodoxy today; the latter activity has even acquired its own space-age and unfortunate title, "retrofitting." Because of changing social patterns and because of their lower energy use, decaying old cities in the northeastern United States, like Boston, New York, Philadelphia, and Cleveland, are now being proclaimed by some people of vision as cities of the future. This prediction is being denied hotly in the newer motor cities of the Sun Belt, like Denver, Houston, Al-

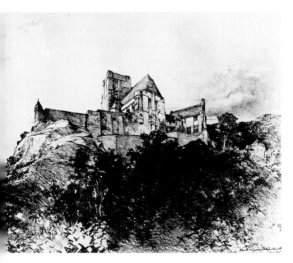

24. Bertram Goodhue's drawing
of the Frederick Peterson House,
Westchester County, New York, 1915.
(Photograph courtesy of John Rivers)

buquerque, and Los Angeles; and for the short run at least, it is also denied by policies of the national administration that took office in 1981.

On the purely stylistic front, it now seems fine to many architects to disregard totally what was once an ultimate taboo of the International Style and to make architecture that recalls buildings from the past or that plays with something of their spirit in a cartoonlike way or that is, perhaps most surprisingly of all, just downright traditional. But also the winds of European fashion, which have periodically sent architectural gusts to us, have reached our shores once again and are now all the rage in some circles. Thus as an alternative to returning to tradition for inspiration, it seems all right to some—altogether grim to others—for buildings to be clothed in the new and astonishingly chaste vestments of Neo-Rationalism.

What could all these supposedly clear but nonetheless diverse developments have in common? One realm in which communality can be sought is in the national spirit of our time, which it is architecture's purpose, or at least fate, to express. This spirit needs to be contrasted to the spirit of times just recently past.

To live or work or grow up in America in the 1950s and early 1960s was for many, if not all, people to crest a wave of virtually unlimited promise. Almost anything seemed within reach. Boundless economic prosperity was at hand, political change seemed possible, social justice was thinkable, and even worldwide peace was at least conceivable. This was an optimistic period in architecture, and one symbol of it was the General Motors Technical Center in suburban Detroit—modern, hygienic, low-rise, low-density, and highly technological buildings set in a primly landscaped campus far from the aging city center (25). This was a time of architecture designed to celebrate the future rather than to sympathize with the past. Vast amounts of building occurred everywhere: schools, colleges, office towers, churches, shopping centers, cultural centers, and even cultural shopping centers, like Lincoln Center in New York. Although the suburbs flourished, many aging city centers languished. Other city centers underwent startling changes. Park Avenue in New York went from a residential street of masonry-clad buildings to a monumental collection of apparently weightless towers of glass and steel. The symbols, indeed, of urban renewal and revitalization were a shimmering glass skyscraper and a travertine cultural center. Slum dwellings by the square mile were demolished by bulldozers with the intention of building vast housing projects designed around utopian precepts of twentieth-century visionaries, and old neighborhoods were sliced brutally in two by new high-speed freeways. This was the better environment that was meant to ensure a bet-

25. General Motors Technical Center,
Warren, Michigan,
by Eero Saarinen, 1953.
(Photograph: ESTO, Ezra Stoller)

ter life, but which in many cases did not. In purely stylistic terms, the International Style was the perfect language for a nation with a new, confident, boastful, and even arrogant view of itself as the leader of the free world.

This giant wave of promise, for many Americans, broke, and broke spectacularly, through a series of economic, political, and military misadventures, plus others that were thrown in gratuitously by fate. Thus by the mid-1970s America as a whole had experienced a severe cultural mood swing, since many promises on many fronts were rudely broken and so many options shut off with a bang, like a series of doors slamming along an endless corridor. Thus the urgent question began to shift from "What will we do next?" to "How can we do something that is right?" or finally at last to "What can we do at all?"

Architecture too seemed to falter. McKim, Mead & White's imperial Pennsylvania Station in New York was demolished and replaced with a banal commercial structure, a seminal event that proved we did not much value our architectural past and also that we could not very easily make something nearly as good. Pruitt-Igo's ambitious housing project of the 1950s in St. Louis was abandoned and blown up, and it became a truly disheartening symbol of the inability of architecture to resolve real social and cultural problems. Even grandiose attempts at urban revitalization seemed to falter, and they still do. The gleaming new Renaissance Center in Detroit (26), for instance, has so far failed to reverse the plight of that city and has even by some estimates polarized the situation by standing in such striking contrast to the surrounding urban decay. Hundreds of places and buildings that in retrospect seem characteristically American have now been replaced by new buildings that seem to characterize nowhere at all. Most recent among the casualties is the small town with its streets lined with trees and sidewalks and houses, which had front porches, and its downtown with a courthouse and often a square. There were once literally thousands of towns designed to this format in the United States (27). But what began in the 1950s and 1960s in the cities has now spread to the provinces, and these towns are now being rediscovered, "revitalized," and ruined.

Powerfully depressing experiences like these, plus cultural shocks like the energy shortage that became apparent in 1973, or the constitutional crisis that occurred in 1974 and led to the resignation of a president, or the ongoing and still underrated crisis of ecology—plus, of course, the not-forgotten Vietnamese War, a divisive event at once so obvious and so dreadful as almost to seem not worth mentioning—have added to and con-

Top:
26. Renaissance Center, Detroit, Michigan, by John Portman & Associates, Phase I, 1977. (Photograph: Gerald Allen)

Above:
27. Elm Street, Lumberton, North Carolina, early twentieth century. (Photograph: Gerald Allen)

firmed the accumulating data that can be summarized in this one plain point: all our resources now seem much more limited than we had once guessed. Among these are not just the physical ones with which we make and do things, not just money and oil and power. Among these now must be included our own collective resources of personal energy, imagination, and intellect, and of judgment, ethics, and vision. But these limits, which are so vividly apparent to many Americans today, are certainly not yet universally acknowledged by all, and indeed are totally rejected by some, because they are so contrary to America's still-surviving myth of itself as a land of limitless opportunity. This fundamental schism and the crisis it presents characterize the present moment.

American architecture today is therefore not so much an architecture that is itself in crisis as it is an architecture *about* crisis. The crisis, that is, is not in architecture; the crisis is in America, and architecture abundantly reflects it. What is being drawn, including most of the contents of this book, is a reaction not just to the architecture of the recent past but also to the culture that made it—and also, of course, to the question of where do we go from here. The answer to this question involves in essence two, and only two, alternative modes of thought and expression: rustic and urban. Each of these alternatives has deep roots in our national tradition and indeed in the most ancient traditions of all humanity.

THE RUSTIC AND THE URBAN

To understand the drawings in our collection it is necessary to develop general concepts through which they can be considered. Let us therefore begin, for purposes of our argument, by assuming that the most fundamental purpose of art in general, and of architecture and architectural drawings in particular, is to be a foil against meaninglessness. This, we will assume, is why art is made and also why it is appreciated. In assuming this we also realize, and we are not the first to note, that we are all born into the world for reasons which we find at least initially unclear, that we live from one fragment of time to another through a course of experiences that could be regarded as essentially random, and that the termination of these events, death, can occur at a moment in the continuum which is gratuitous. Thus the experience of life, when we consider it this harshly, presents the specter of meaninglessness.

But the human mind has its own defenses against this frightening apparition. Obvious among them are its resources of conceptualization and of memory. The mind's power to form concepts is its ability to organize phenomena into patterns that are empirically coherent and that have the potential of being observed again in the future as having repeated themselves. The power of memory is the ability to recall these patterns and to recall as well patterns that other people have formed. Also obvious among the mind's resources is its vision of human purpose, though this is difficult to account for. Is it simply based on an observation of what has worked best in the past (and therefore a function of conceptualization and memory), or is it based on inherent ideals of what ought in any case to be? In either event, nevertheless, the vision of purpose does exist.

Therefore, the defense that the mind attempts to erect against the threat of meaninglessness is its opposite, meaning. The failure in any one particular person's mind to succeed in this attempt would be one way of defining madness. The collective ability of a group of minds to achieve at least tolerable success would be a way of defining civilization, with its resulting structures of moral, ethical, social, political, economic, and many other orders—by no means the least of which are science and technology.

Among these structures, of course, is the structure of art. In art a strict selection of human experiences is made from a vast and essentially random array, and this selection is then composed into ordered artifice—physical and permanent in the case of material art and nonphysical and recurrent in the case of nonmaterial art. By doing this, art achieves meaning. Part of such meaning lies in the nature of the artifact itself. We have earlier described this, for instance, in the case of the church of San Estevan in New Mexico (1), with its implication of the endurance of things, or in the case of the string quartet that never exists as a whole, with its suggestion of recurrent creation. Another and much more obvious part of the meaning that a work of art embodies lies, of course, in its particular formal and its thematic contents.

We propose that the formal and thematic content of all art, including architecture and therefore architectural drawings, can be encompassed within only two concepts, urban and rustic. Urban involves the idea of the town, and rustic, of course, has to do with the idea of the country. But both concepts are capable of great richness.

The idea of the town, for instance, includes the notion that people can live together in close proximity and interdependence, and therefore it implies the existence of social, economic, and political structures. Since there are worse and better versions of all these structures, the notion of progress from the former to the latter emerges, as does the notion of urbanity itself, which, as everybody knows, involves the idea not just of a town, but of a sophisticated one. So too, by contrast, emerges the notion of revolution, which is a radical way of speeding up the advancement of things along the urban scale of progress. What is foremost among all these ideas, however, is the concept of human reason and the rational, intellectual pursuits, including science and technology, which govern the development of all the urban phenomena mentioned so far. Therefore, the idea of what is urban emphasizes the ideas of society, economics, politics, progress, urbanity, revolution, science, technology, and reason.

The idea of the country, by contrast, contains very nearly all the opposites of the idea of the town. Individual self-reliance replaces society, self-sufficiency replaces economics, laissez-faire replaces politics, cyclical repetition replaces progress, unpretentious naturalness replaces urbanity, evolution replaces revolution, intuition replaces science and technology, and the imagination replaces the faculty of reason. Independence replaces interdependence.

It is obvious that cities—at least traditional ones like New York, if not newer ones like Los Angeles—are mainly urban and that the countryside is mainly rustic. But further examples are less simple. Anarchy, for instance, as a mode of social behavior in cities is a rustic concept, just as agriculture, a carefully organized way of making the earth productive for human use, is an urban notion. Central Park in New York is a rustic form, while the national grid that divides much of the United States into regular segments is an urban one. The Farnsworth House by Ludwig Mies van der Rohe and Fallingwater by Frank Lloyd Wright are both in rural settings, yet the former is urban in essence and only the latter is rustic. Geometric ornament, wherever it occurs in architecture and the decorative arts, is urban; botanical ornament is rustic. The concept of what is urban and the concept of what is rustic provide two separate and quite distinct pathways toward meaningful perceptions of the world and meaningful representations of it. They are alternatives in the true sense, since neither is completely preferable to the other and since both are of proven efficacy in humanity's historic attempt to understand itself and its predicament. They are usually regarded as being locked in conflict, though it would be more accurate to note that they are more often in unstable solution—possibly in all of human culture, but certainly in Western European culture, and particularly in that of England. But nowhere else is the instability of the solution more apparent than in America, whose initial European enthusiasts in the seventeenth and eighteenth centuries fell into two very different camps and whose current native boosters still do to some extent. On the one hand, there was one group of Europeans who saw in America a natural, perfect Eden waiting for the taking and free from the corrupting structures of European culture; these were the primitivists. On the other hand, there was another group who saw it as a setting where human reason could begin now to produce social, economic, and political progress; these were the liberals and progressives. The blending of these two incompatible points of view helped create the resultingly somewhat inconsistent idea of what America was. The late historian Richard Hofstadter once wrote that America was "the only country in the world to begin with perfection and aspire to progress." Another way to put this succinct appraisal, in our terms, would be to say that America began with the rustic and aspired to the urban.

In American architecture, rustic and urban themes, and also rustic and urban forms, have always been melded together. The suburb—which is arguably an exclusively Anglo-American invention—is mainly rustic, with housing and other domestic aspects of the urban environment transposed into the semblance of an Arcadian setting. The architecture of the International Style—"modern" architecture—is mainly urban, with its passions for rationality, technology, social progress, and even revolution. Here the rustic enters in for the most part as neatly cultivated parks and plazas that fill the spaces between the buildings themselves.

The collection of new American architectural drawings shown in this book continues this now-honorable tradition of mixing the rustic and the urban. Many illustrate the rustic propensities for individuality and intuition, and perhaps even more importantly they rely on the recall of forms remote enough from the present and native enough to our past to seem almost natural in our landscape, and in the process they reveal a belief in the cyclical evolution of things rather than in revolutionary progress. Others, of course, are veritably supermodern in their rational and revolutionary urban preoccupations. The majority, however, vacillate somewhere in between, just like the culture from which they spring.

PART 2

THE DRAWINGS

CESAR PELLI

Right:
Corporate Headquarters Building,
Pittsburgh, Pennsylvania
Perspective
Stabilo on paper
24 x 16 inches (61 x 41 cm.)

Below:
Corporate Headquarters Building,
Pittsburgh, Pennsylvania
Perspective
Stabilo on paper
6 x 3 inches (15 x 7.5 cm.)

After many years of working within the structures and traditions of other firms, I opened my own architectural office in 1977. This new office started and grew around certain design intentions, and it was natural and desirable to develop or adopt drawing techniques that suited those intentions and that represented my work and that of my new firm.

The drawings are made with a wax-based pencil (Prismacolor or stabilo). Each pencil stroke is generally diagonal. The diagonal lines introduce a level of order that allows many hands to work upon a single drawing. The precision of each drawing may vary depending upon the discipline within which the diagonal stroke is maintained. Each line is layered upon the other to build density and to control value.

This drawing style is a particularly appropriate representation of my own architecture. It is primarily an expression of surface and volume as contrasted to other kinds of drawings that represent lines. We use the same drawing technique for plans, elevations, and perspectives. Our drawings are representational, not analytical; they are intended to communicate the ideas of the buildings. Surface, light, shadow, and volume—all qualities of the finished buildings—can be easily expressed within these drawings. This technique can also suggest many of those unpredictable perceptual qualities of the architecture, such as reflections and transparency.

I first learned this drawing technique at the office of Eero Saarinen and Associates. Jay Barr, one of Eero's partners at that time and one of the best draftsmen I have known, used it best and most often. The technique is basically the same as that used by Eliel Saarinen in his drawing for the Chicago Tribune Competition in 1922. Everybody in our firm can now use it. Because we now use it for every purpose, it is acquiring great richness, and it becomes more adaptable every day. It is now part of the personality of our firm and our work.

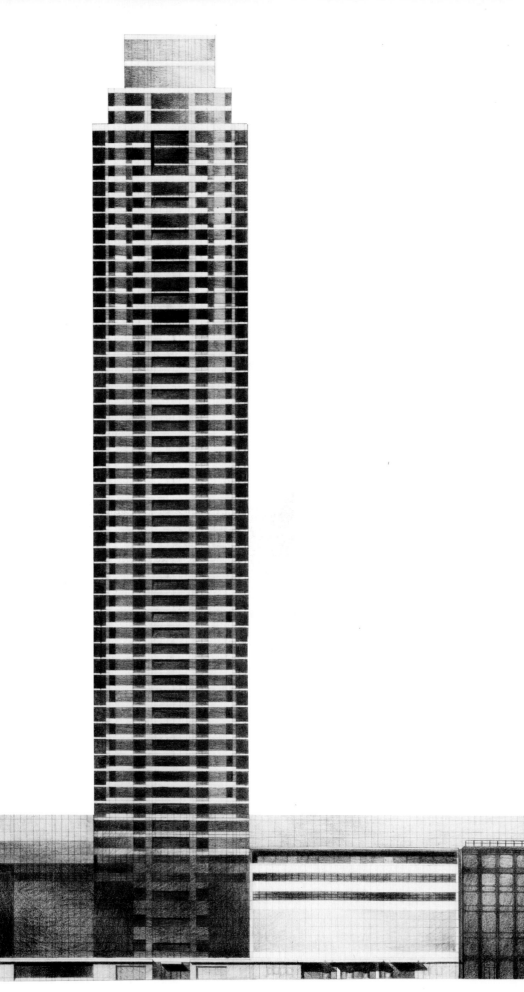

CESAR PELLI

The Museum of Modern Art Expansion
and Museum Tower, New York
Elevation
Colored pencil on black line print
72½ x 49½ inches (184 x 126 cm.)

Right:
Long Gallery House
Axonometric
Stabilo and Prismacolor on paper
16 x 10 inches (41 x 25 cm.)

Below:
Long Gallery House
Axonometric
Colored paper collage
16 x 10 inches (41 x 25 cm.)

Long Gallery House
Elevation
Stabilo and Prismacolor on paper
12 x 50 inches (30 x 127 cm.)

THOMAS BEEBY

Right:
The House of Virgil
Perspective
Magic Marker on yellow tracing paper
36 x 36 inches (91 x 91 cm.)

Below:
Bahamas House
Perspective
Magic Marker on drafting linen
39 3/8 x 27 9/16 inches (100 x 70 cm.)

The drawings represent the poetic intentions of the architecture itself. They are completed with mundane materials and methods familiar to all architects—Magic Marker applied to an ink image traced from a roughly constructed pencil sketch. The goal is to unlock the veiled fantasy that is always present, to transcend material description by evoking the symbolic basis of architecture.

Symbols are shared by architect, client, and society, and sometimes they transcend society and culture to touch on archetypal forms of a spiritual nature. Recognizable and evocative figures from the past appear as indicators of the relationship of the architecture to humanity and to nature. Color is used as a vehicle of subjective response to produce drawings that represent an architecture of pure sentiment.

MICHAEL SORKIN

Familiar techniques of representation embody characteristic distortions in response to the need to present in two dimensions something proposed for three. Despite consistent accuracy of scale, I dislike the uniform angularity of axonometric projection, as well as its overlay of modernist cachet. Perspective, with its fudged dimensions, mainly strikes me as too hokey. I like, however, the quality of image and information given in plan, section, and elevation. That traditional mode is at once measurably reliable and can be rendered illusory, the best of both worlds.

The drawings presented here are done in pencil, a medium that appeals for its malleability and cleanliness. At the time they were done I was interested in a pretty pale range of colors, which has, alas, unfortunate consequences for reproduction.

One submission for the "Late Entries" to the Chicago Tribune competition is a skyscraper organized along classic tower lines: base, shaft, and top. Its imagery is drawn from Deco, from aeronautical forms, and from the literal-minded sexuality long associated with skyscrapers. My intent, however, was to create a more androgynous object by including female elements more conspicuously. Thus the entryway, for example, is flanked by bisected airliner forms that resolve themselves into breasts. The flames that emanate from the top are meant to contrast with a companion project that spouts water. A second entry in the Tribune competition is mainly concerned with an investigation of the second major skyscraper paradigm, the slab. Here the solution is a division into a series of slipping slabs. A cascade of water falls down landscaped roof terraces and is channeled into a large glass tube through which it descends to the ground, powering a clock. A large electric sign gives the news. Blowing trees and spray reveal that we are in the Windy City.

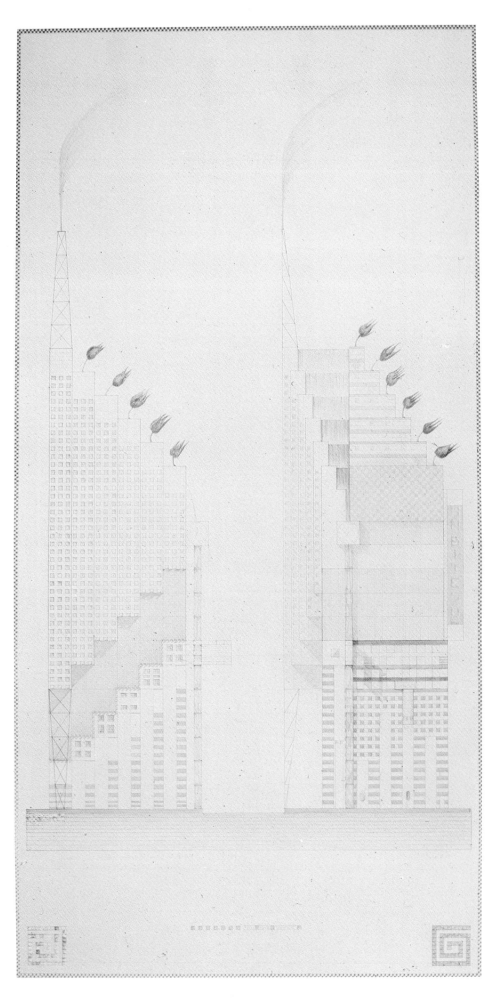

Chicago Tribune Tower Competition/
Late Entries
Elevations
Verithin pencils on Strathmore paper
60 x 30 inches (152 x 76 cm.)

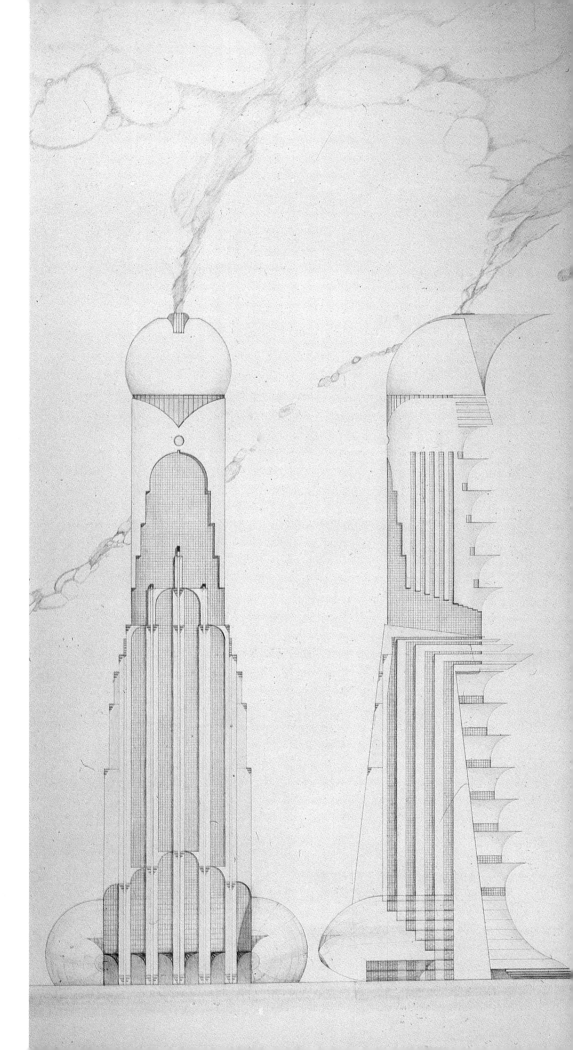

HENRY MELTZER AND RICHARD OLIVER

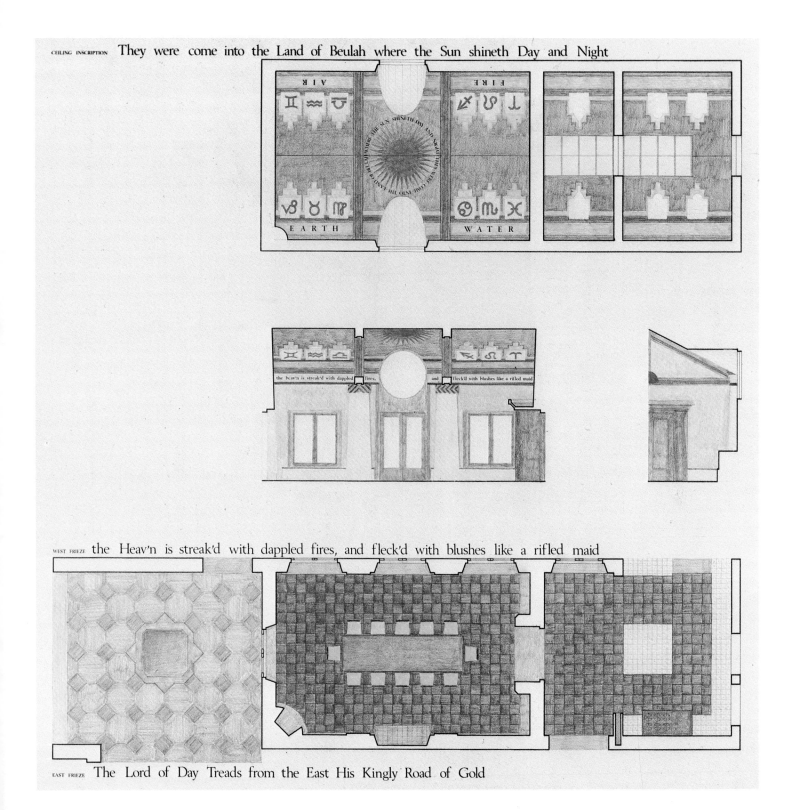

CEILING INSCRIPTION They were come into the Land of Beulah where the Sun shineth Day and Night

WEST FRIEZE the Heav'n is streak'd with dappled fires, and fleck'd with blushes like a rifled maid

EAST FRIEZE The Lord of Day Treads from the East His Kingly Road of Gold

The plan of the Dewey House project is drawn to distinguish clearly the additions and remodelings from the existing parts, even though the old and new portions would not have been so distinct in actuality. The inspiration for this graphic depiction of the plan came from the drawings of Sir Bannister Fletcher, which elegantly trace the various campaigns by which great cathedrals acquired their present form. Ink on Mylar allows the graphic clarity needed in this type of drawing.

The major new room in the Dewey House project is the dining room. A program of art and symbolism was proposed for the surfaces of the room. This drawing depicts the surfaces rather than the space of the room at a scale large enough to include the ornamental details. The use of Prismacolor pencils provides a softer, more impressionistic drawing in addition to the depiction of color.

The elevations of the project were drawn to show the integration of old and new construction. The soft, pictorial technique using Prismacolor pencils on yellow tracing paper was inspired by the drawings of Michael Graves.

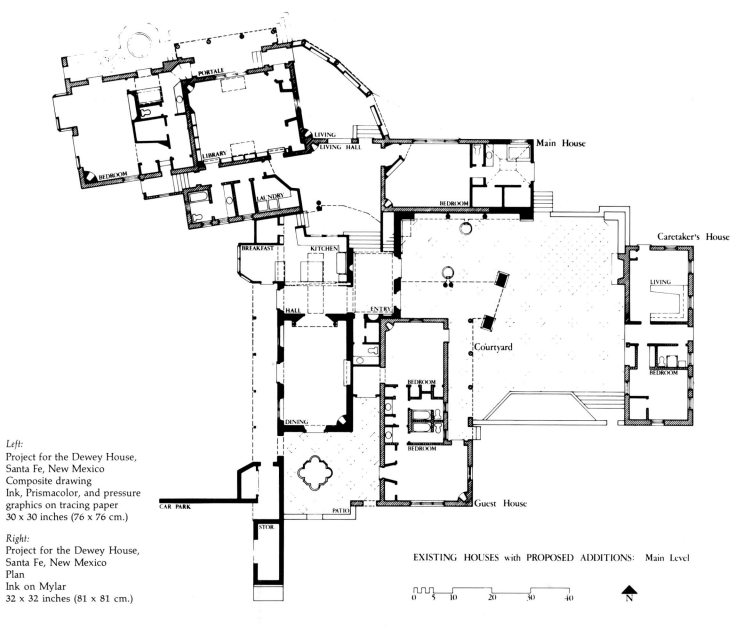

Left:
Project for the Dewey House,
Santa Fe, New Mexico
Composite drawing
Ink, Prismacolor, and pressure
graphics on tracing paper
30 x 30 inches (76 x 76 cm.)

Right:
Project for the Dewey House,
Santa Fe, New Mexico
Plan
Ink on Mylar
32 x 32 inches (81 x 81 cm.)

EXISTING HOUSES with PROPOSED ADDITIONS: Main Level

0 5 10   20   30   40

N

Project for the Dewey House,
Santa Fe, New Mexico
Elevations
Prismacolor on yellow tracing paper
16 x 32 inches (41 x 81 cm.)

BARTHOLOMEW VOORSANGER AND EDWARD I. MILLS

Our firm's system of drawings is intended to aid in the exploration of ideas and images in architecture. The drawings are a continual graphic exploration within this context. The individual types of drawings, like the axonometric, unfold and reconnect planes and spaces in a visual continuum; the color elevations augment study of architectural layers that we separate by color, and the one-point perspectives offer the unique advantage of allowing the individual to gather all the space and plans together into a single focus. Although some of the drawings are produced intentionally as presentation documents, all these drawing systems named above are used in the development of visualizing and validating ideas prior to the actual building process.

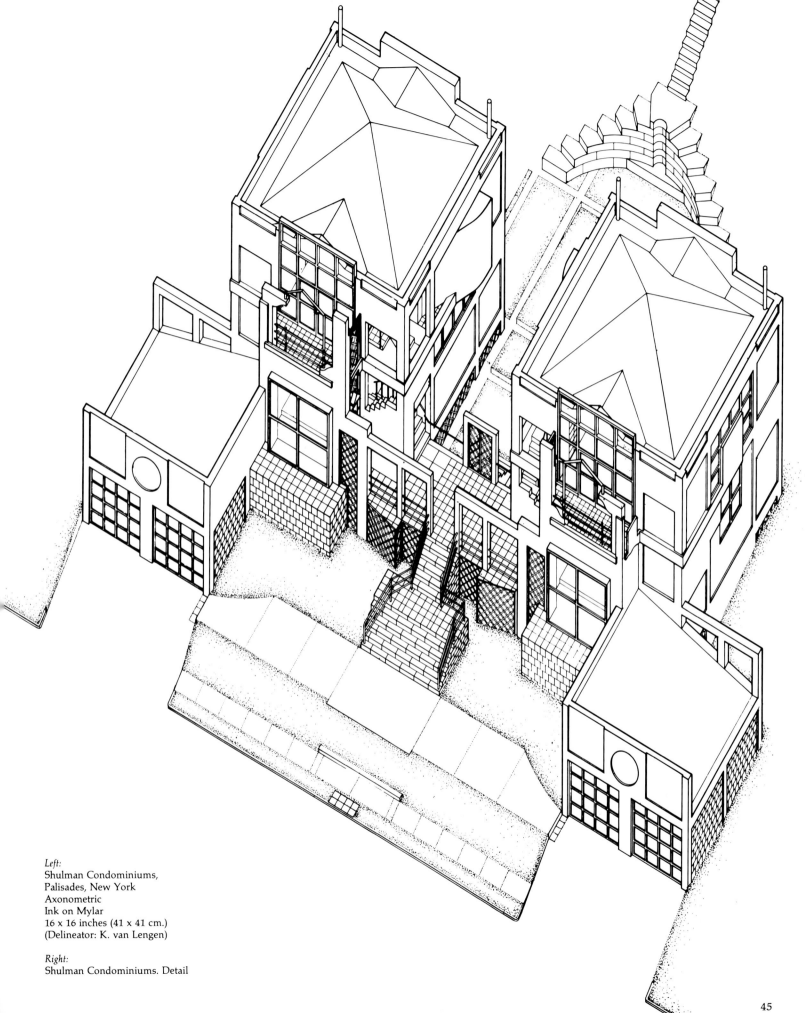

Left:
Shulman Condominiums,
Palisades, New York
Axonometric
Ink on Mylar
16 x 16 inches (41 x 41 cm.)
(Delineator: K. van Lengen)

Right:
Shulman Condominiums. Detail

Sanpaolo Bank of Turin offices, New York
Axonometric
Ink on Mylar
16 x 16 inches (41 x 41 cm.)
(Delineator: J. Holland)

BARTHOLOMEW VOORSANGER AND EDWARD I. MILLS

Sanpaolo Bank of Turin offices, New York
Perspectives
Ink on Mylar
16 x 16 inches (41 x 41 cm.)
(Delineator: E. Mills)

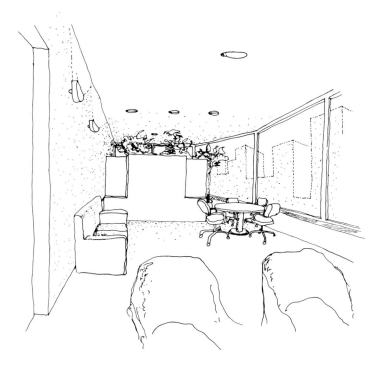

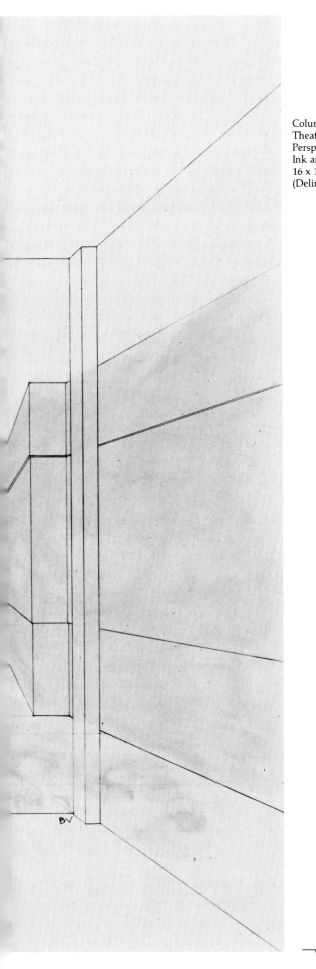

Columbia Broadcasting Company
Theatrical Film Division offices, New York
Perspective
Ink and Prismacolor on vellum
16 x 16 inches (41 x 41 cm.)
(Delineator: R. Velsor)

Columbia Broadcasting Company
Theatrical Film Division offices, New York
Axonometric
Ink on Mylar
11 x 6 inches (28 x 15 cm.)
(Delineator: R. Velsor)

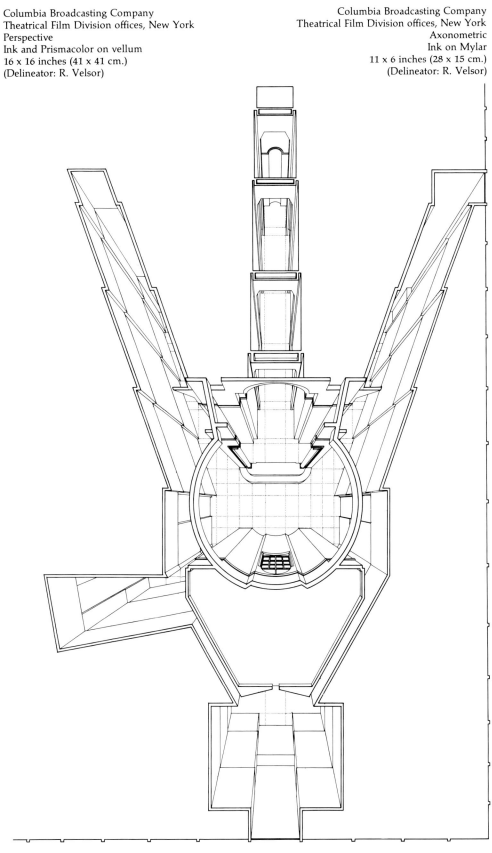

JAMES COOTE

Most of the drawings were done freehand in pencil on heavy white tracing paper (yellow seems to distract me). I like the graphite's softness, suggestiveness, and responsiveness in both sketches and presentation drawings. I do color studies mainly on small Xerox reductions, which allow quick studies of many possibilities. Though I use many kinds of views, I rely heavily on perspectives, which I find useful for conceptual abstractions, as well as for imitations of appearance, often based on slides of the site. I like images that evoke atmosphere and character, perhaps more than those that describe geometry or intellectual organization.

Approach, Browder House,
Austin, Texas, 1981
Perspective
Pencil on white tracing paper (Albanene)
23 x 34 inches (58 x 86 cm.)

JAMES COOTE

Browder House, Austin, Texas, 1981
Axonometric
Pencil on white tracing paper
23 x 25 inches (58 x 64 cm.)

View from existing allee, Kilgore House,
Austin, Texas, 1981
Perspective
Pencil on white tracing apper (Albanene)
20 x 30 inches (51 x 76 cm.)

Study of living room with "Adam" ceiling,
Kilgore House, Austin, Texas, 1981
Composite drawing
Pencil on white tracing paper
14 x 17 inches (36 x 43 cm.)

Study of fireplace corner,
David-Peese House,
Austin, Texas, 1979
Perspective
Pencil on white tracing paper (Albanene)
4¼ x 4¼ inches (11 x 11 cm.)

Interior of great hall,
David-Peese House,
Austin, Texas, 1979
Perspective
Xerox of original pencil
on white tracing paper (Albanene),
with colored pencil
8½ x 11 inches (22 x 28 cm.)

DANIEL LIBESKIND

Architectural drawings have in modern times assumed the identity of signs; they have become the fixed and silent accomplices in the overwhelming endeavor of building and construction. In this way their own open and unknowable horizon has been reduced to a level that proclaims the a priori coherence of technique. In considering them as mere technical adjuncts, collaborating in the execution of a series made up of self-evident steps, they have appeared either as self-effacing materials or as pure formulations cut off from every external reference.

There is a historical tradition in architecture, whereby drawings (as well as other forms of communication) signify more than can be embodied in stabilized frameworks of objectifiable data. If we can go beyond the material carrier (sign) into the internal reality of a drawing, the reduction of representation to a formal system—seeming at first as void and useless—begins to appear as an extension of reality that is quite natural. The system ceases to be perceived as a process whose coherence is supported by empty symbols and reveals a structure whose manifestation is only mediated by symbolism.

An architectural drawing is as much a prospective unfolding of future possibilities as it is a recovery of a particular history to whose intentions it testifies and whose limits it always challenges. In any case, a drawing is more than the shadow of an object, more than a pile of lines, more than a resignation to the inertia of convention.

The act of creation in the order of procedures of imagination, here as elsewhere, coincides with creation in the objective realm. Drawing is not mere invention; its efficacy is not drawn from its own unlimited resources of liberty.

I am interested in the profound relation that exists between the intuition of geometric structure as it manifests itself in a preobjective sphere of experience and the possibility of formalization that tries to overtake it in the objective realm. In fact, these seemingly exclusive attitudes polarize the movement of imagination and give an impression of discontinuity, when in reality they are but different and reciprocal moments—alternative viewpoints—of the same fundamental ontological necessity.

My work attempts to express the inadequacy at the heart of perception for which no (final) terms are provided—a lack of fulfillment that prevents manifestation from being reducible to an object-datum. Only as horizons, in relation to time, can forms appear in this exploration of the "marginal" where concepts and premonitions overlap. There is a presentation, but always according to the mode of imperfection, an internal play in which deferred completeness is united with a mobilized openness. The work remains an indefinite series because this dialectic cannot be halted. As such, these drawings and collages develop in an area of architectural thinking that is neither a physics nor a poetics of space.

Most of all, however. I am a fascinated observer and a perplexed participant of that mysterious desire which seeks a radical elucidation of the original precomprehension of forms—an ambition that I think is implicit in all architecture. If there is true abstraction here (as opposed to generalization), it is not achieved by the elimination of contents through a gradual deployment of an increasing emptiness, but is rather an isolation of structural essence whose manifestation in two dimensions illuminates all the subsystems of projection (for example, three-dimensional space).

Right:
Micromegas: "The Burrow Laws"
Composite drawing
Silk screen on paper
36 x 26 inches (92 x 66 cm.)

Pages 62–63:
Micromegas: "Leakage"
Composite drawing
Silk screen on paper
26 x 36 inches (66 x 92 cm.)

Page 64:
Micromegas: "Maldoror's Equation"
Composite drawing
Silk screen on paper
36 x 26 inches (92 x 66 cm.)

Page 65:
Micromegas: "Vertical Horizon"
Composite drawing
Silk screen on paper
36 x 26 inches (92 x 66 cm.)

Pages 66–67:
Micromegas: "Dance Sounds"
Composite drawing
Silk screen on paper
26 x 36 inches (66 x 92 cm.)

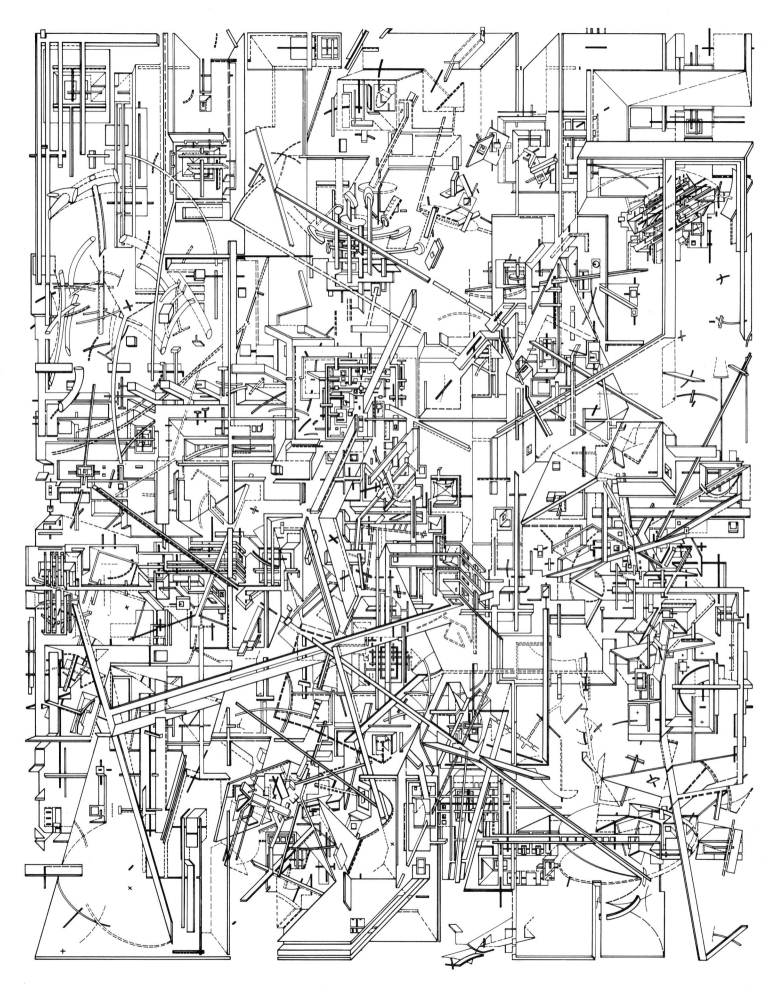

61

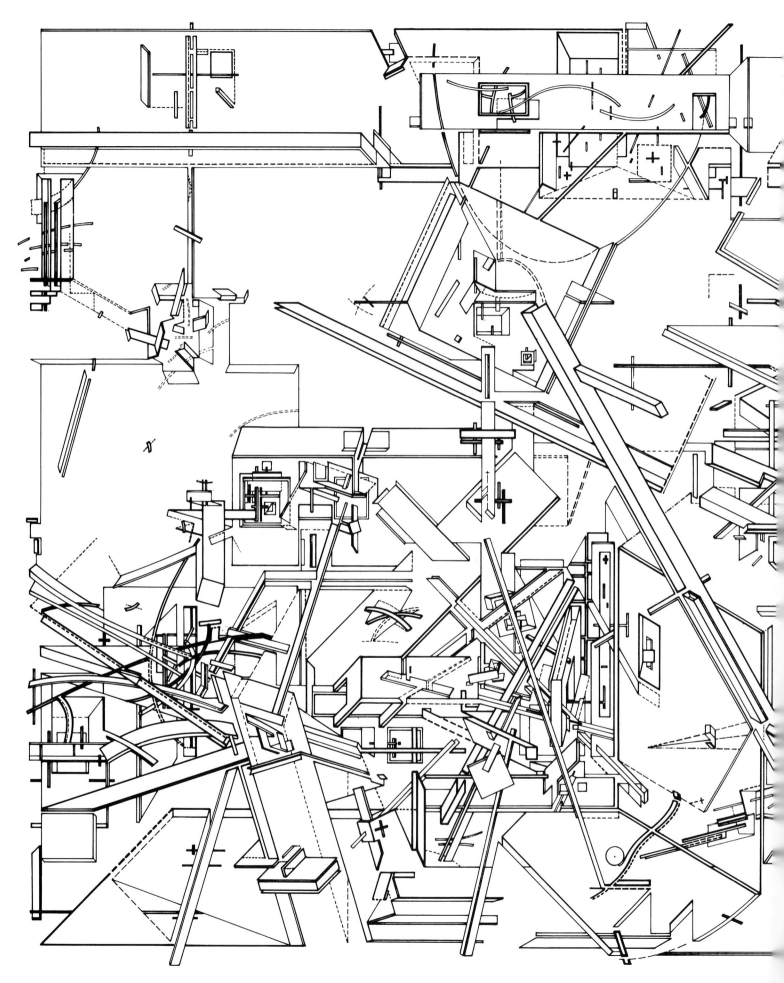

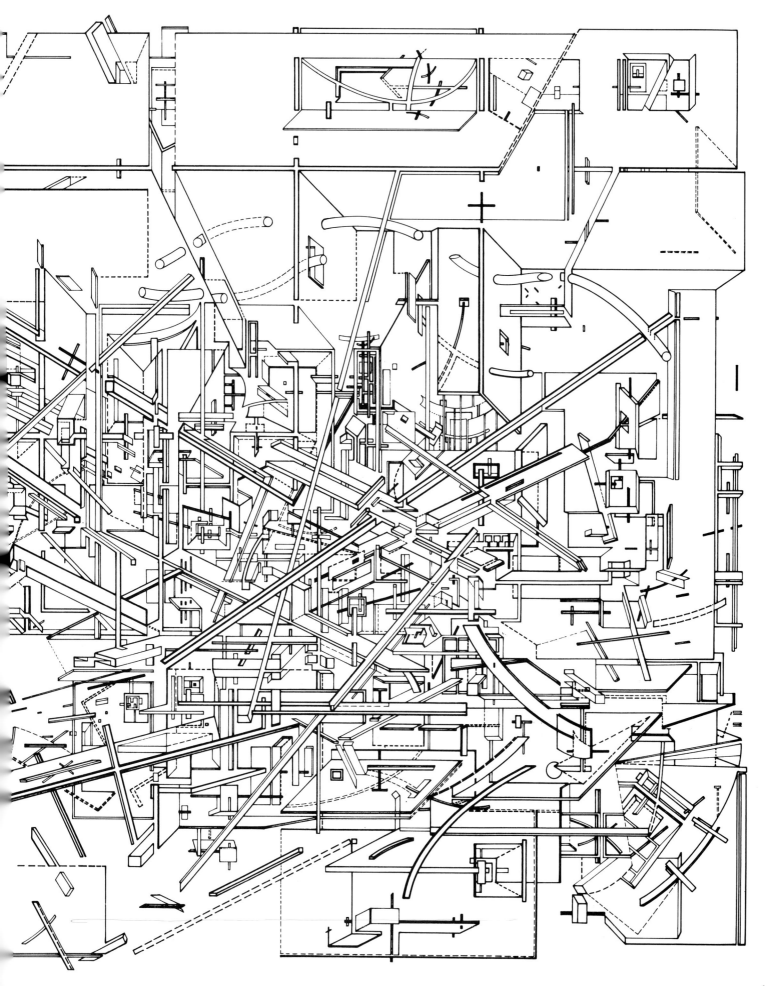

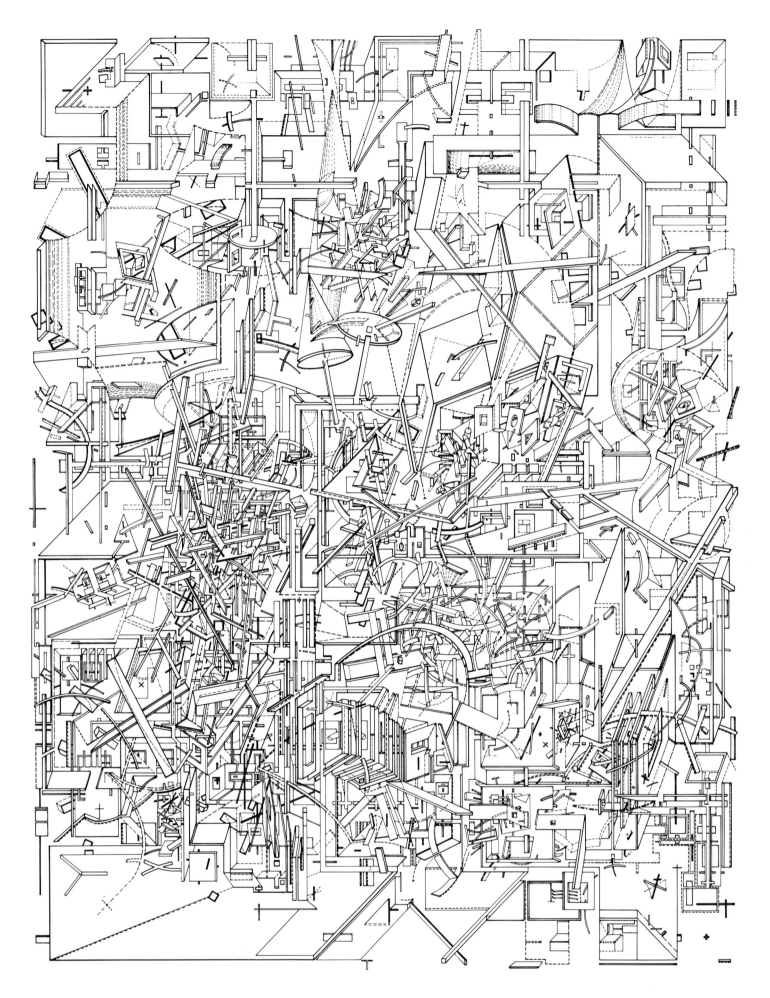

64

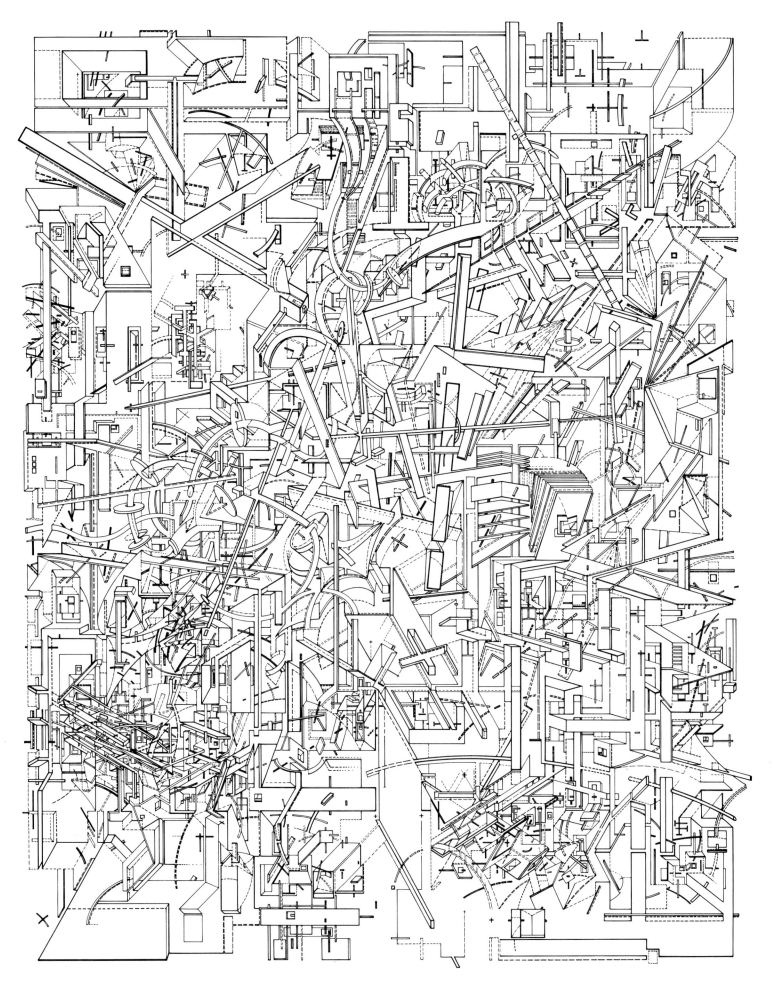

65

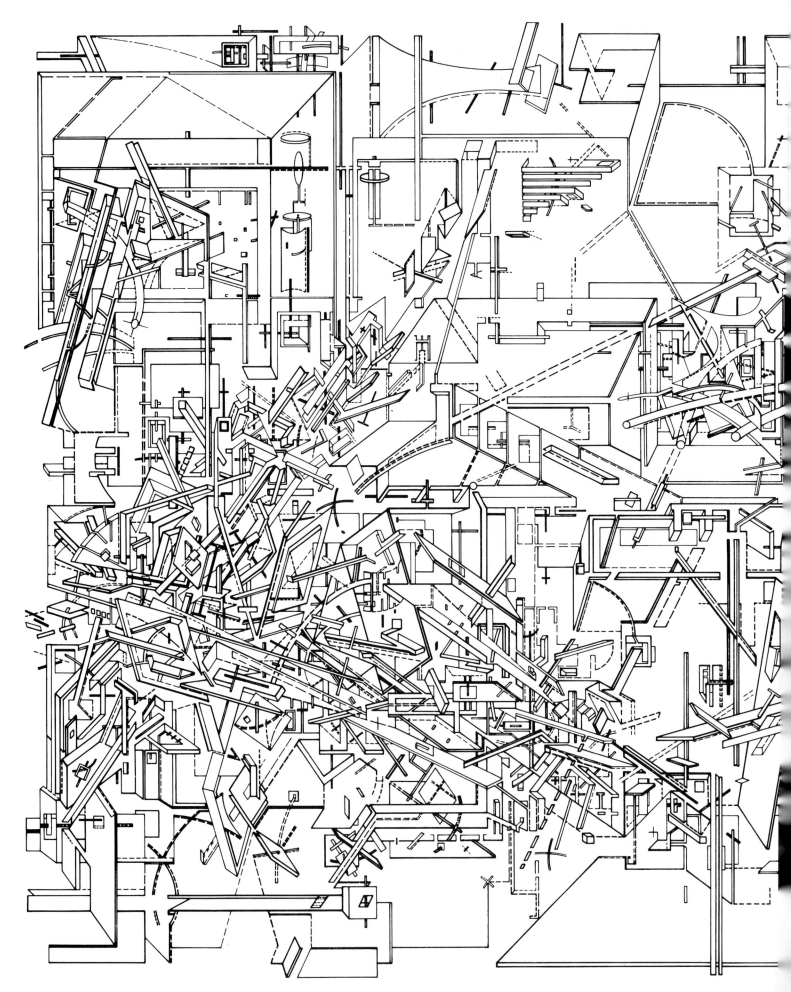

66

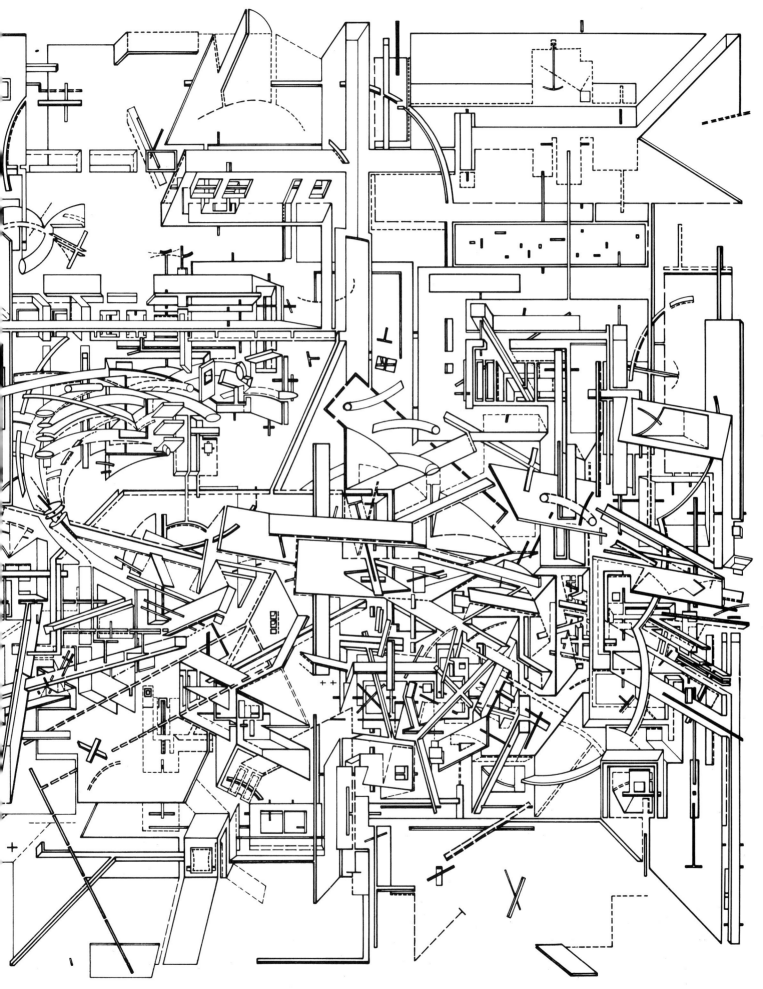

RODOLFO MACHADO AND JORGE SILVETTI

The technique and rhetorical mechanisms utilized in the drawing of the living room with fireplace represent the function of the room through an attribute. If we consider the basic envelope of the room, it could be read as a two-point perspective; if we focus on the fireplace, the attribute of the room, the drawing is seen as a frontal, symmetrical, one-point perspective. The drawing of the house on the Island of Djerba shows a straightforward facade. As part of the set of four facades, organized clockwise, it depicts unmistakably the spatial armature of the building: the stair wrapping around the cube or, conversely, the cube being revealed by the unwrapping of the stair. The drawing of the facade of the Country House is a strongly colored—almost "Roman" and *"fauve"*—conspicuously skyless, contextless vertical projection that seemed the most suitable channel for the embodiment of some of the ideas that informed the design—for instance, the author's desire to design a piece typologically clear and powerful. It is a critique and a proposal, and consequently it is a self-assertive, rather aggressive drawing rendered with short, gestural, and controlled pencil strokes. In a word, the discourse of drawings (the iconic discourse) and the discourse of ideas (the ideological discourse) are unavoidably linked. The perspective of a bedroom in a country house is a one-point, pure line, sectional perspective where the main intent has been the description of the composition of the interior. Metaphorically, it is the kind of ordered argument that does not admit shadings. "A Theory of the Production of Architecture" is a drawing of drawings. It began as a recollection, a self-analysis, and also an investigation of techniques of representation at all levels. It is, figuratively, a collage of forms from our projects, but more importantly it is a collage of modes of representation.

Living Room, Country House, 1977
Perspective
Pencil on rag paper
15 x 14¾ inches (38 x 37 cm.)
(Designer: Rodolfo Machado;
Delineators: Rodolfo Machado and Tarek Ashkar)

Steps of Providence, 1978–1979
Perspective
Ink on Mylar
18 x 20 inches (46 x 51 cm.)
(Designers and Delineators:
Rodolfo Machado and Jorge Silvetti)

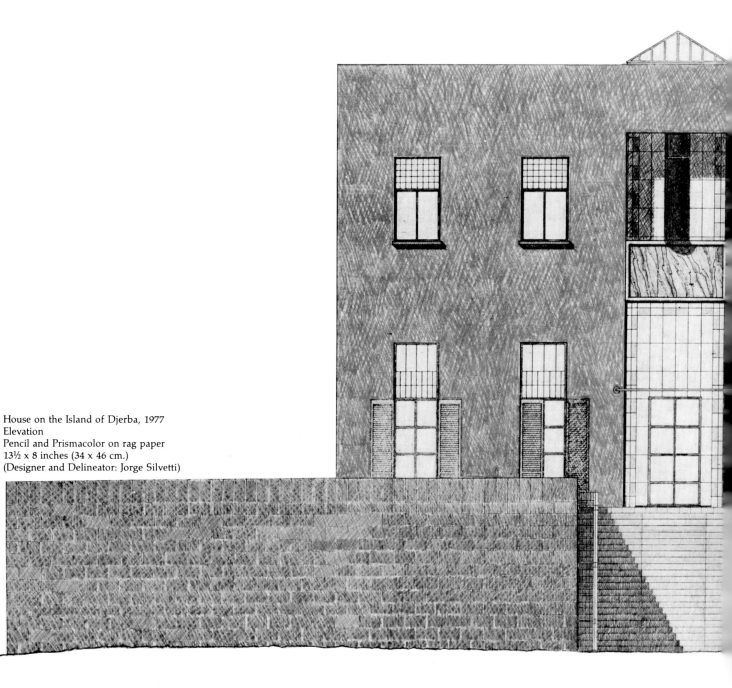

House on the Island of Djerba, 1977
Elevation
Pencil and Prismacolor on rag paper
13½ x 8 inches (34 x 46 cm.)
(Designer and Delineator: Jorge Silvetti)

Country House, 1977
Elevation
Prismacolor on rag paper
15 x 24½ inches (38 x 62 cm.)
(Designer: Rodolfo Machado;
Delineators: Rodolfo Machado and Tarek Ashkar)

A Theory of Production of Architecture
Composite drawing
Prismacolor on rag paper
40 x 30 inches (102 x 76 cm.)
(Designers: Rodolfo Machado and Jorge Silvetti;
Delineator: Jorge Silvetti)

Bedroom, Country House, 1977
Perspective
Pencil on rag paper
15 x 14¾ inches (38 x 37 cm.)
(Designer: Rodolfo Machado;
Delineators: Rodolfo Machado and Tarek Ashkar)

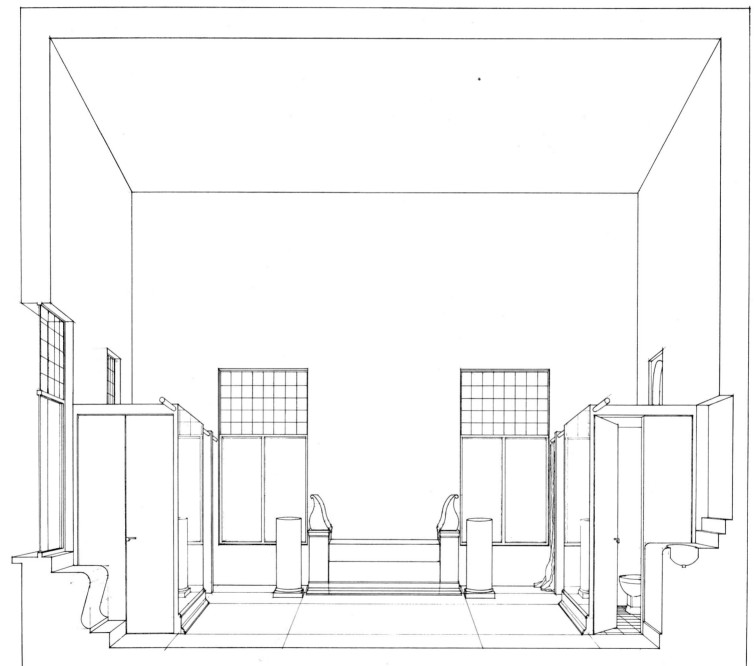

HELMUT JAHN

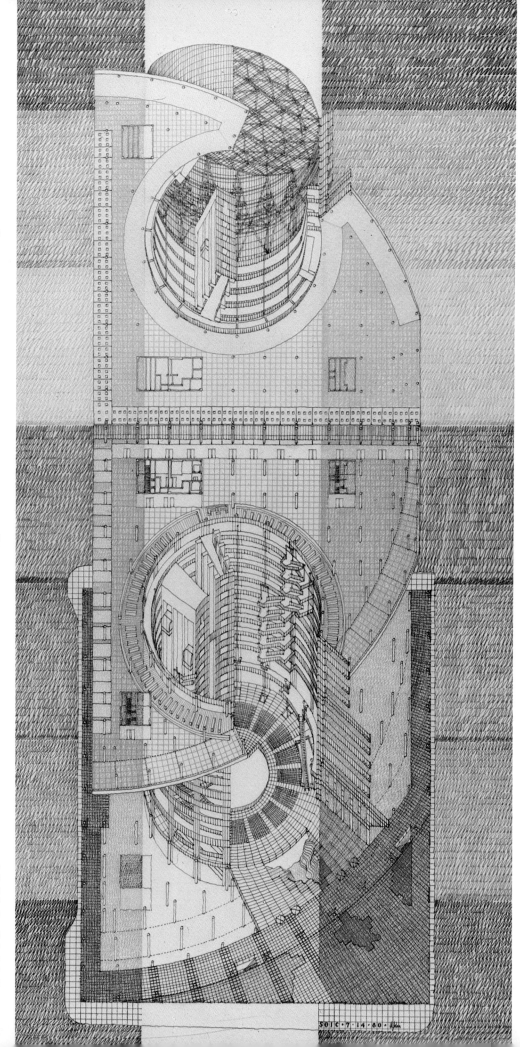

The drawings illustrate the State of Illinois Center at Chicago, an assembly of technology, image, urban design, and historical symbolism. They use two techniques that are representations of basic prototypes: the orthographic projection and the axonometric.

The axonometric projection offers the best simultaneous representation of plan and elevation and also the best perception of three-dimensional space on a two-dimensional plan—though still not the same as reality. It is simultaneously concerned with perception and expression, and it describes both exterior and interior space. It allows us to proceed to an investigation of its parts from an understanding of the building's whole. The plan view explores the elements of the base, while the reflected plan examines the elements of the top. The color of the background is representative of the polychromatic character of the various building elements.

The orthographic projection allows the rendition of the vertical and horizontal planes in a composition that reveals all the elements of the building in truthful dimensions: the arcade, the plan, the structure, the central space, the circulation elements, and the top. The rays of light emanating from the space are indicators of a world-of-tomorrow ambience. The gradations in the colors of the earth and sky are representative of the polychromatic character of the various building elements.

Both drawings express, in their complexity, the multiple images and conceptual and aesthetic ideals of the building. The style of the drawings is linked to the style of the architecture, with the conscious concern that it is the building that matters at the end.

Right:
State of Illinois Center, Chicago, Illinois
Axonometric
Ink and colored pencil on tracing paper
60 x 30 inches (152 x 75 cm.)

Opposite page:
State of Illinois Center, Chicago, Illinois
Orthographic projection
Ink and colored pencil on tracing paper
50 x 40 inches (127 x 102 cm.)

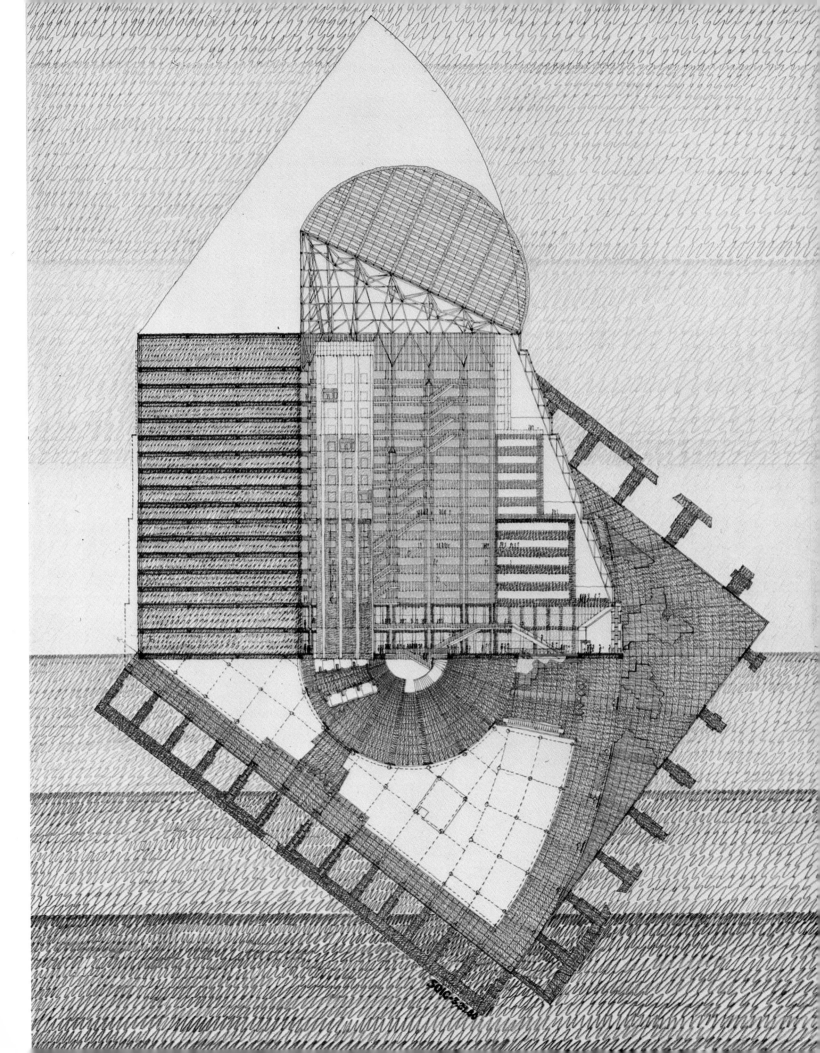

LAURETTA VINCIARELLI

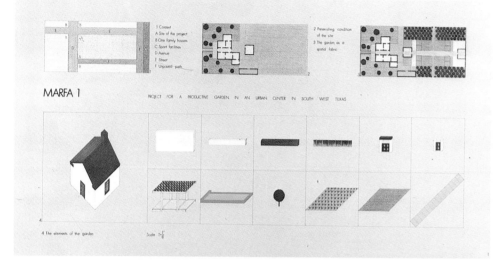

MARFA 1   PROJECT FOR A PRODUCTIVE GARDEN IN AN URBAN CENTER IN SOUTH WEST TEXAS

The selection and invention of appropriate means of representation have always been part of my research in architecture. I think that the relationship between means of expression and architectural content is always ambiguous, always not exhaustive, above all when projects are multilayered in meaning. The graphic conventions at the same time clarify and obscure spatial meanings. The representation through perspective and conceptual drawing is always something else than built architecture. It is always about it, never it.

Looking again today at these drawings of 1978, I am aware that the representation of the garden reflects first of all my consciousness of that project at that time and that today I would represent it somewhat differently. I would substitute for the axonometric drawing of the garden two perspectives along the axis, so that the quality of the designed space, which is a perspective space, would emerge clearly. Also my debt to the early Italian Renais-

sance would be more fully acknowledged.

This garden contains architectural themes that continue to be present in my work today. It is in fact through furthering the theme of the spatial fabric and the exploration of the role of the measuring element—which appears here as the axial pergola—that what was unconscious before appears clear now, and other representations of the garden seem possible to me.

The use of the color reflects the chromatic environment of the garden. Trees and greens are abstracted in shape to emphasize their function as architectural elements through which, in fact, the garden is organized and defined. In this presentation, the plan assumes a particular importance due to the mainly horizontal nature of the spatial relationships. Their minute description in plan permits the reading of this architecture as mainly created by horizontal surfaces that are juxtaposed and differently textured.

Left:
Marfa 1, Marfa, Texas
Composite drawing
Ink and Prismacolor on vellum
23¼ x 41½ inches (59 x 105 cm.)

Below:
Marfa 1, Marfa, Texas
Axonometric
Ink and Prismacolor on vellum
23¼ x 41½ inches (59 x 105 cm.)

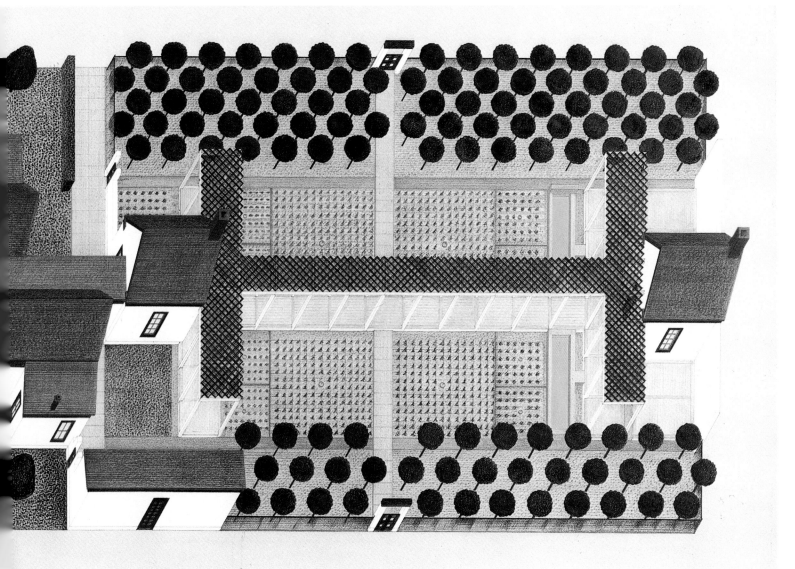

F. ANDRUS BURR

The drawings show my interest in an architecture of formalism and an architecture of the sublime. At the same time, I am trying to be particularly American by borrowing from nineteenth-century classicism, from the vernacular, and from the Shingle Style. The drawings alternate between two-dimensional and three-dimensional representations. This is a reflection of my simultaneous interests in the composition of plan and elevation, on the one hand, and in the sculptural and experiential aspects of architecture, on the other. Each drawing is a description of a building that exists in my mind, though I do not try to make them literally accurate. I want the drawings to have a quality of their own—the dream quality of imagined buildings.

DePeyster House

A CABIN IN THE STANLEY BASIN

Cats in the street
Perspective
Ink and watercolor on paper
12 x 9 inches (30 x 23 cm.)

People often ask me if I see what I draw and if I would be interested in perfecting certain drawing techniques to portray more accurately the subjects drawn. My objective is to create a feeling of place for the viewer, to give him or her my subjective slant on the scene.

The point of view that I use in my drawing is a composite of available vignettes seen when standing in a space. The streetscapes are sketched while standing on a street, on rooftops, or on an overpass. I have tried to use photographs as a reference, but I find that memory assigns priority in a way better suited to evocative final drawings. When you are able to see a landscape or streetscape in a drawing showing more detail, or from an angle you wouldn't be able to see in reality, the scene can communicate more to you even at a subliminal level than more traditional views. Another deliberate aspect of my drawing technique is that of line and plane. The kind of line I use and its irregularity are an attempt to communicate an immediacy about the subject. I violate the rules of perspective regarding lines and planes to show the viewer how quirky and special the area in a drawing is and how, in my imagination, the street could be filled with hats in celebration of its uniqueness.

Unusual colors are also applied in a loose watercolor technique. The colors are drawn, in part, from places where people paint and embellish buildings in traditional ways. The blotchiness of the watercolor application reminds us that even the surface of the paper participates in the character of the final drawing.

Congratulations!

you knocked their cats in the street.

Hats in the street
Perspective
Ink and watercolor on paper
12 x 9 inches (30 x 23 cm.)

Urban vignette I
Perspective
Ink on paper
12 x 9 inches (30 x 23 cm.)

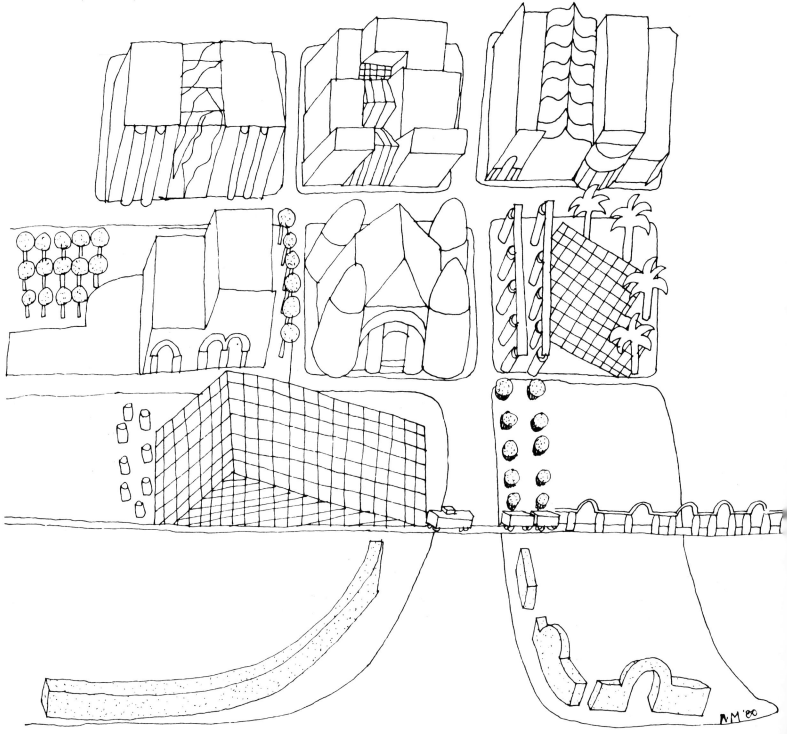

Urban vignette II
Perspective
Ink on paper
12 x 9 inches (30 x 23 cm.)

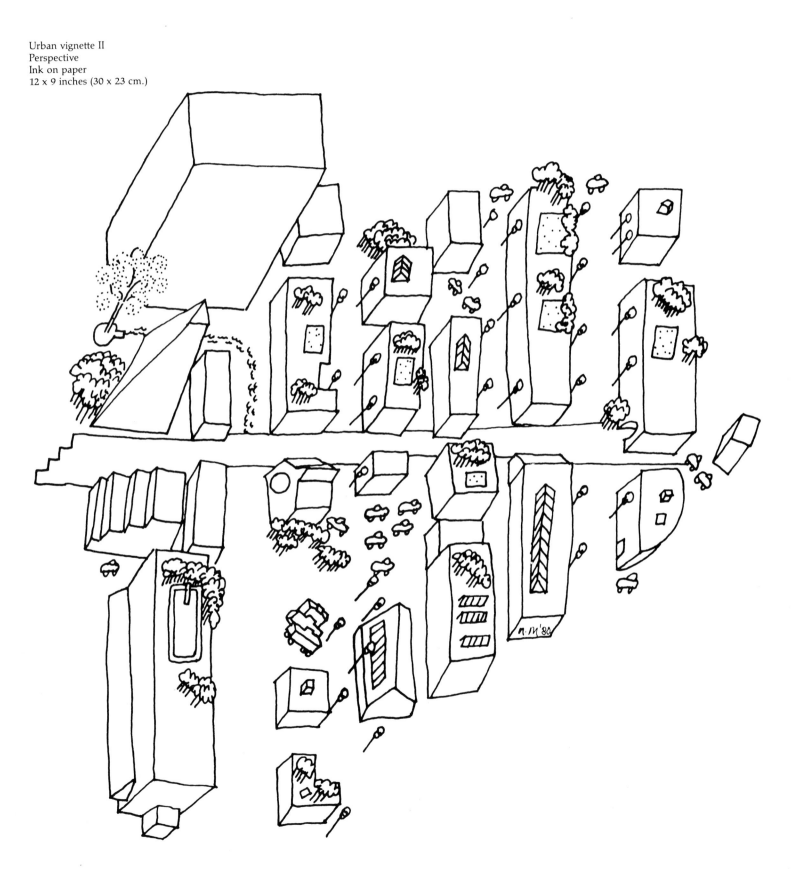

Panorama with John Tatum's building
Perspective
Ink and colored pencil on paper
22 x 36 inches (56 x 91 cm.)

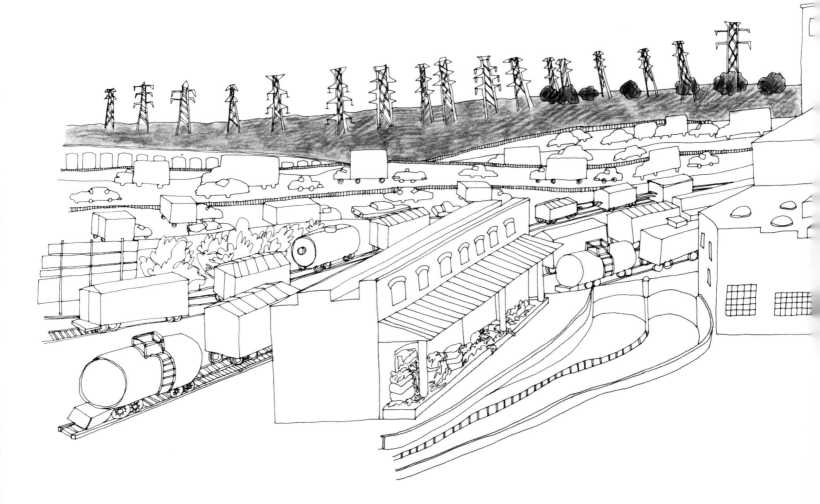

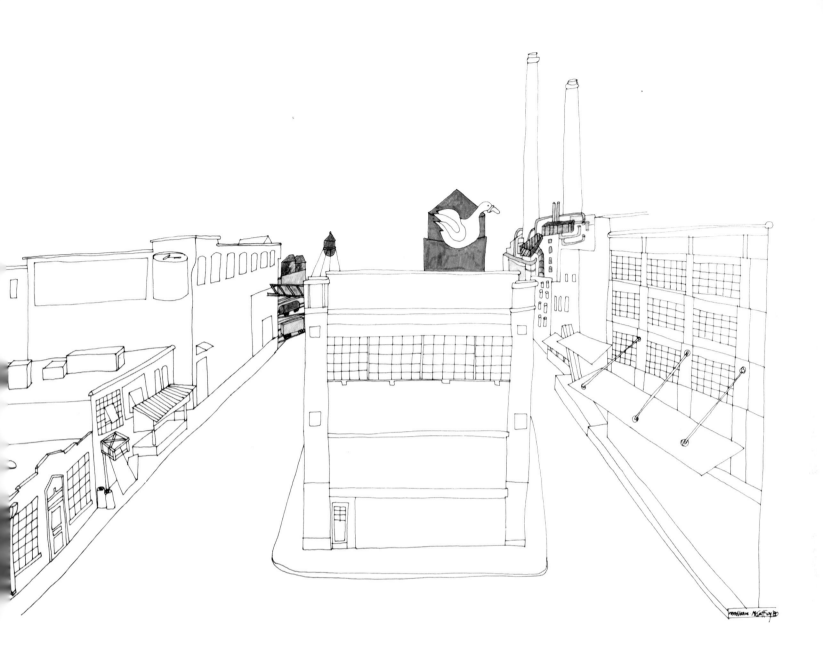

Invisible cities I
Perspective
Ink on paper
12 x 9 inches (30 x 23 cm.)

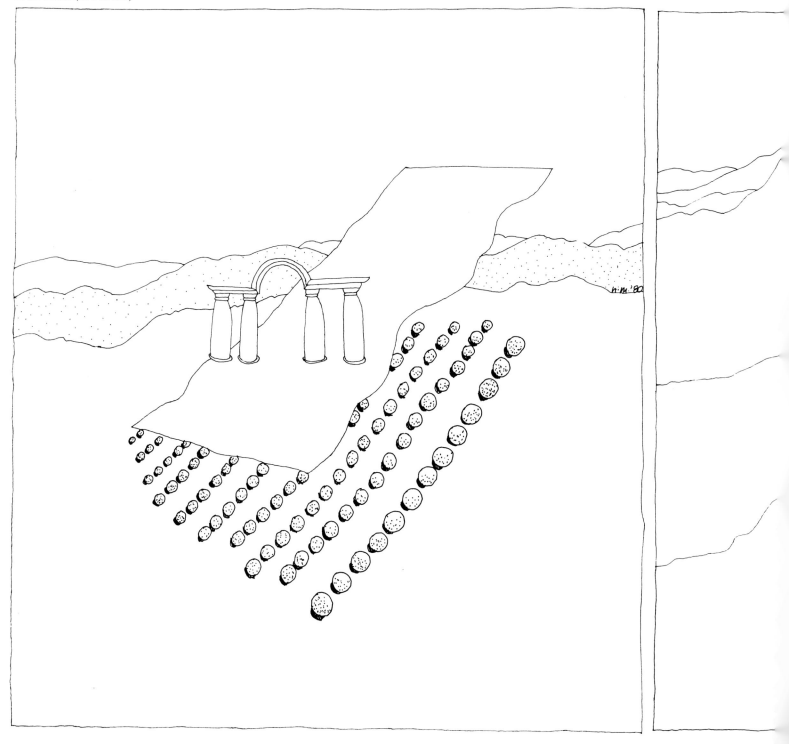

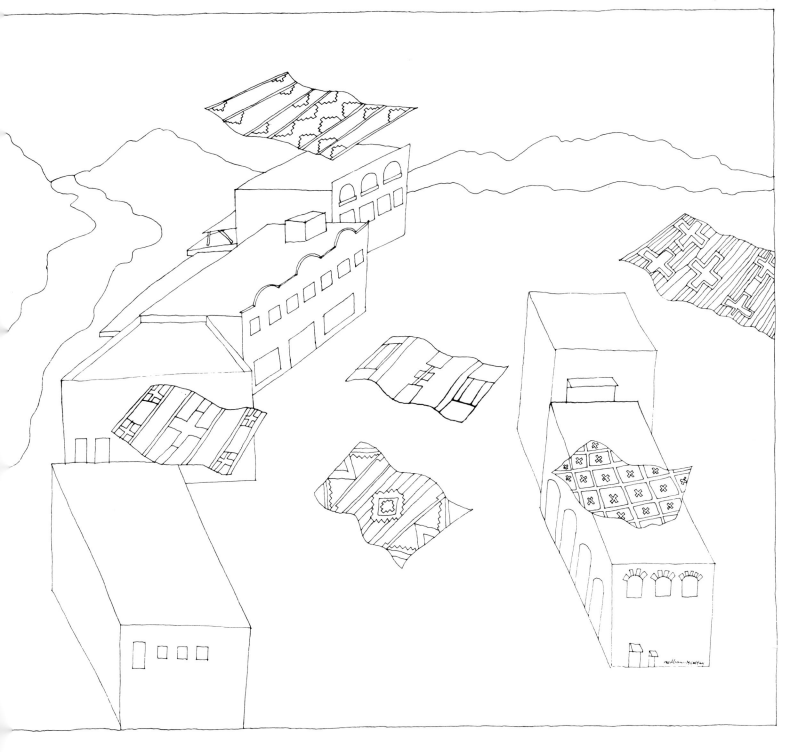

Rug over building
Perspective
Ink on paper
9 x 12 inches (23 x 30 cm.)

ROBERT A. M. STERN

Drawing is a means of communication about architecture; it is at once an *imitation* of previous realities and an *intimation* of realities to come. Perhaps even more than an actual building, the architectural drawing is a record of one's intentions at the moment of design. While I record my architectural ideas at the level of conceptualization by means of a quick sketch scrawled on tracing paper, on the back of an envelope, on a napkin, on whatever is handy, I do not make the drawings that frequently communicate to the public my architectural intentions and the intentions of my collaborators in the office. Quite frankly, I don't draw that well; but then, neither am I a master carpenter or stonemason. Nonetheless, I have lots of ideas about drawings, just as I do about the properties and possibilities of wood and stone. I am also a good listener; so I listen to the carpenter's or mason's idea about how to do one thing or another. So too do I work with those among my collaborators in the office who have prepared various drawings of our work. These drawings, then, like the architectural ideas they represent, are the products of collaboration—not the collaboration of Gropius's ideal team, but a give and take over empty coffee cups and paper-strewn desks at late hours when the phone has at last stopped its ringing.

I believe that techniques of drawing relate not only to the delineator's individual talent, but also to the ideas being delineated and the role the drawing is expected to play. Thus, seemingly dissimilar projects are drawn in a similar way to make explicit my feelings about their interconnectedness. For example, projects that deal with archetypal images, such as the houses for the Subway Suburb or the prototypical facade for Best Products, are depicted in a flat, highly stylized way to emphasize the explicitly imagistic character of the work.

Similarly, other projects that explore subtler issues of decoration and composition are drawn with fine lines and delicate washes of color in accord with the values intended in the final product. Of course, some projects combine both qualities, as well as others, at once intended as icons and vessels, and so frequently many different ways of drawing will be employed in the study process. As each project is drawn in a variety of ways and different aspects are studied, each new drawing reveals a new set of problems to be addressed in the process of design.

In my own conceptual drawings, I concentrate on the plan and the quick elevation that usually and quite suddenly gets transmogrified into a perspective sketch, the former two testing an organizational structure against measurable standards, the latter confirming or not the capacity of that idea to establish an appropriate character. These drawings are very personal things to me, not the stuff of art, which always has an implication of public communication. Though they play a vital part in my design process, like the many study models we make in the office, they are essentially ephemeral in nature (though I confess that they are saved, just as the models are photographed). In any case, what you see of ours in this book is intended to make a point about the work after its direction has been established; it is intended to crystallize the character of an architectural idea, to keep a kind of vigil for architect and client alike during the arduous and frequently confusing process of making working drawings, letting contracts, and building buildings. It is the icon that keeps the faith; we hope our buildings will be better than our drawings of them, but at the very least the drawings provide a record of our intentions, a standard for measure.

Right:
Residence at East Hampton,
New York, 1980
Plans and elevations
Ink on Mylar
36 x 24 inches (91 x 61 cm.)

Page 90:
Residence at East Hampton,
New York, 1980
Composite drawing
Ink on Mylar
36 x 24 inches (91 x 61 cm.)

Page 91:
Residence at East Hampton,
New York, 1980
Perspectives
Ink on Mylar
36 x 24 inches (91 x 61 cm.)

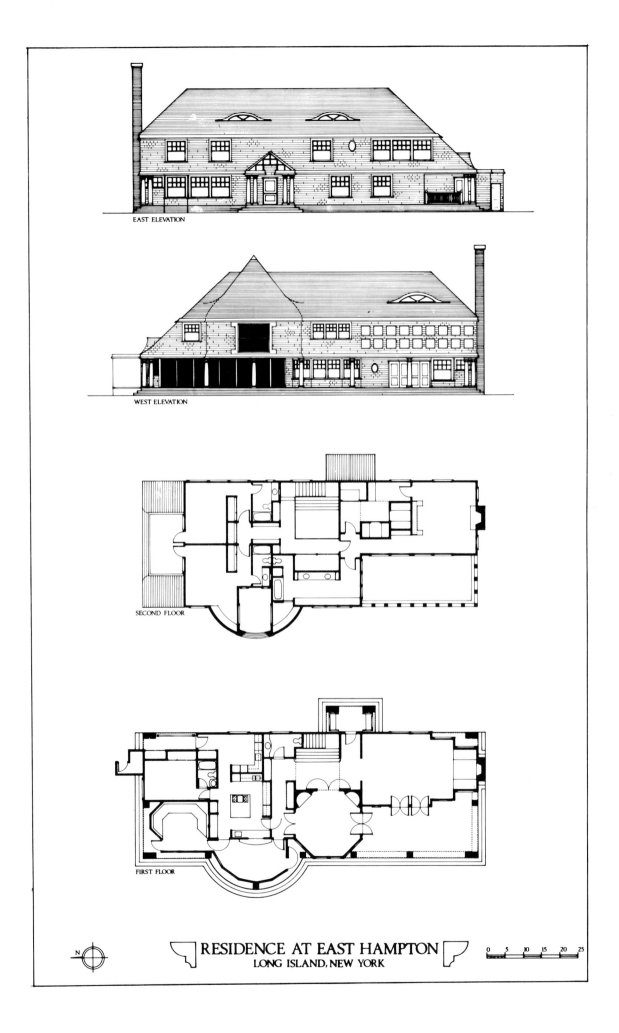

EAST ELEVATION

WEST ELEVATION

SECOND FLOOR

FIRST FLOOR

RESIDENCE AT EAST HAMPTON
LONG ISLAND, NEW YORK

N

0 5 10 15 20 25

SECTION THROUGH TOWER

ELEVATION OF TOWER

NORTH ELEVATION OF HOUSE

ELEVATION AND SECTION OF SCREEN WALL

SECTION OF TOWER WALL

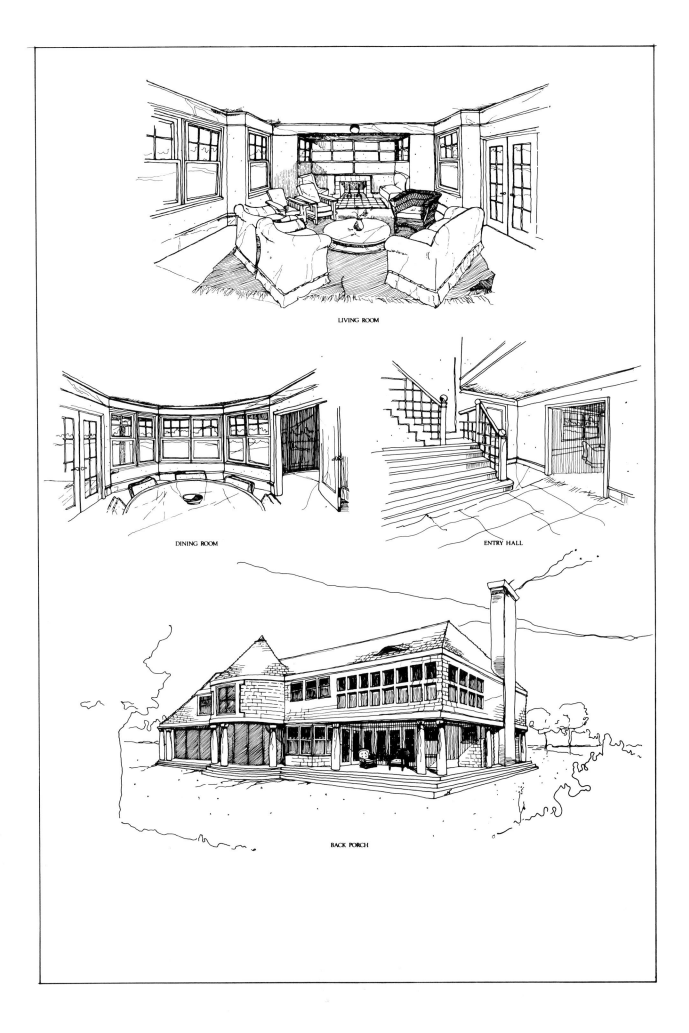

LIVING ROOM

DINING ROOM

ENTRY HALL

BACK PORCH

Right:
Residence in Glen Cove,
New York, 1980–1981
Perspectives
Ink on Mylar
36 x 24 inches (91 x 61 cm.)

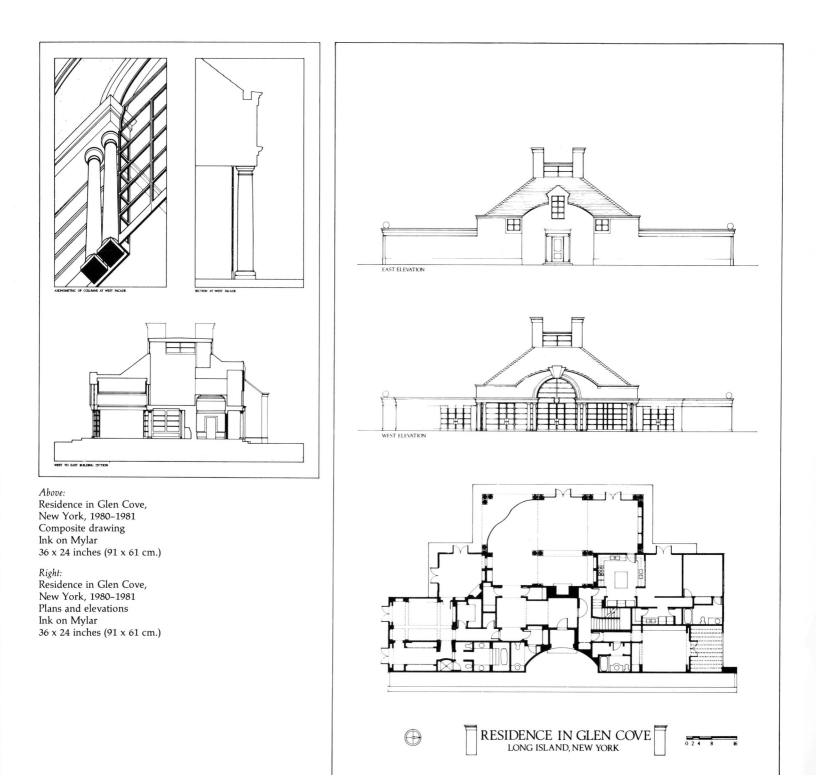

Above:
Residence in Glen Cove,
New York, 1980–1981
Composite drawing
Ink on Mylar
36 x 24 inches (91 x 61 cm.)

Right:
Residence in Glen Cove,
New York, 1980–1981
Plans and elevations
Ink on Mylar
36 x 24 inches (91 x 61 cm.)

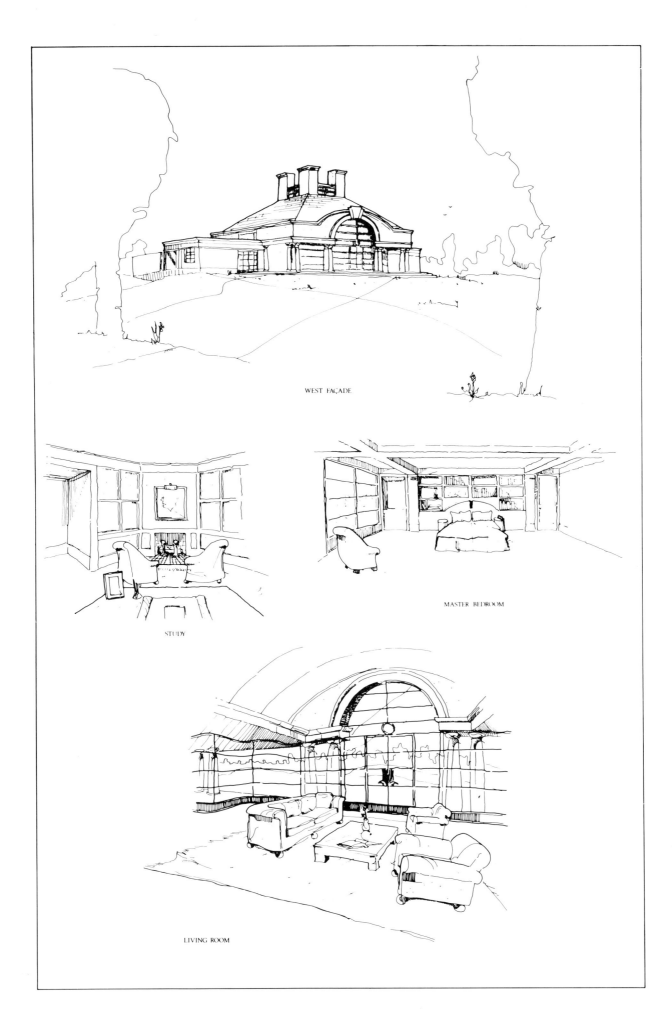

WEST FAÇADE

STUDY

MASTER BEDROOM

LIVING ROOM

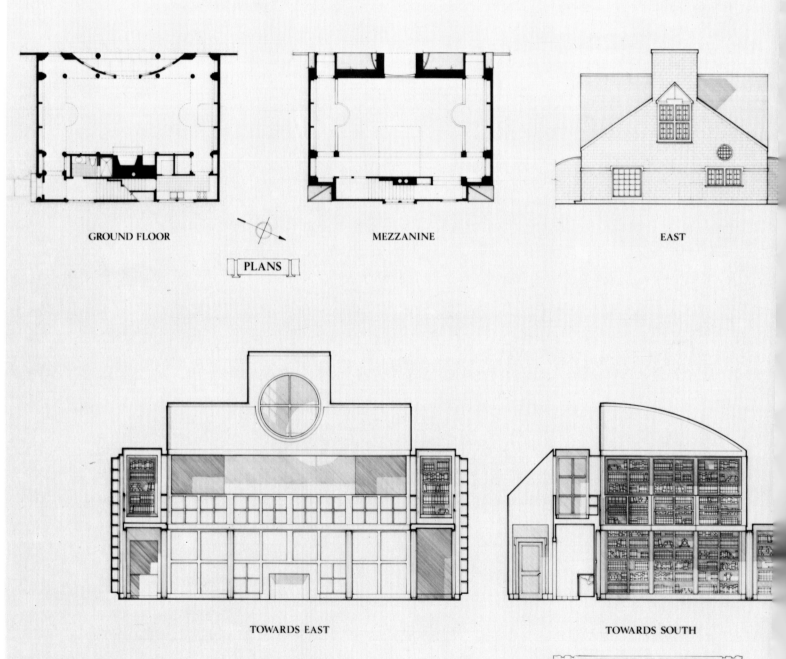

GROUND FLOOR   MEZZANINE   EAST

PLANS

TOWARDS EAST   TOWARDS SOUTH

INTERIOR ELEVATIONS

STUDIO

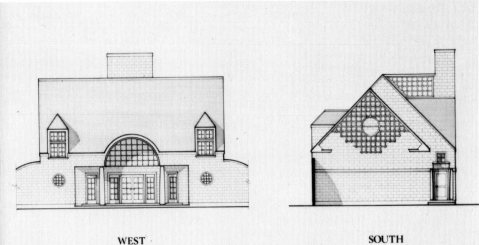

WEST   SOUTH

Studio at East Hampton,
New York, 1979
Composite drawing
Ink on Mylar
24 x 36 inches (61 x 91 cm.)

ELEVATIONS

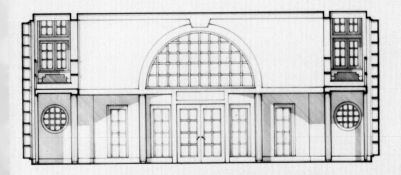

TOWARDS WEST

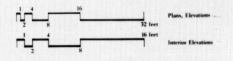

Plans, Elevations

Interior Elevations

TAFT ARCHITECTS

The use of three-dimensional constructions and models as an extension of traditional drawing techniques is an important aspect of Taft Architects' design approach. At the initial stages of a project, small-scale diagrammatic models are used to investigate various possibilities in formal and spatial clarity. As a project develops, larger ones are used to explore more detailed aspects of space through color, patterning, and other studies. The two examples shown here are reconstructions of working models used in the design process. The technique selected for each model is a means for studying specific issues. For this reason the two examples differ in their attitude about space.

The YWCA construction technique allows for particular study of the main space that occurs between three masses. The forced perspective used in the model enables the viewer to become more involved by being part of the space. Multiple vanishing points are introduced in this construction, with the resulting depth foreshortened to about one-third the actual proportional distance.

The model for the Municipal Control Building at Quail Valley is an exploration in a planar progression of space, originating outside the built structure and continuing into the interior of the building. The proportion of the spaces between the layers or implied planes in the model is diminished so that relationships can be studied more clearly.

The use of the diorama, or "shadow box" technique, also allows a degree of control of the space around the model. For display purposes this keeps the model from being viewed solely for its sculptural qualities as an object in space. The box also becomes a container for shipment.

YWCA Downtown Branch and
Office Building, Houston, Texas
Shadow-box model
Glazed tile, wood, chipboard,
Pantone paper, and paint
11 x 17 x 9 inches (28 x 43 x 23 cm.)

Municipal Control Building,
Missouri City, Texas
Shadow-box model
Glazed tile, wood, chipboard,
Pantone paper, and paint
11 x 17 x 9 inches (28 x 43 x 23 cm.)

GERALD ALLEN

The drawings shown here are examples of a quick and relatively easy technique I have recently fallen into the habit of using because it suits many needs at once. All were laid out in pencil roughly and quite large—say, three or four feet wide—then firmed up, again in pencil, and then inked with a felt-tip pen. The results were next reduced photographically to film negatives not more than eighteen or so inches wide, and from these contact prints were made on translucent Mylar. These last are the "originals." They can obviously be made over and over again, and with their thin black lines floating on pearly white backgrounds they seem to impress clients, and I like them too. They also make it, if just barely, on the exhibition circuit, though most potential buyers are put off when they are told that what they see are not really originals. These same Mylar prints also reproduce well—though the special line quality and background vanish—in magazines and books and newspapers with a simple line shot. Even though the lines are thin, they survive crude reproduction processes and further reductions because they are all about the same weight and can therefore be uniformly over-exposed by the copying camera.

All the drawings shown here illustrate finished designs. The ones for Central Park in New York were done before construction of the projects to show what they were intended to look like; the ones of the house in New Jersey were done after construction to show, for various publications, things that photographs could not show—in this case an internal staircase and an exterior view almost completely obscured by trees. I also, of course, make sketches of projects when they are being designed, but these are usually so crude and hapless that I am sometimes embarrassed to show them to the people who work with me, much less in public.

100

Left:
A rustic shelter,
Central Park, New York
Perspective
Contact print on Mylar
12 x 12 inches (30 x 30 cm.)
(Delineator: Michael Barclay)

Below:
A rustic shelter,
Central Park, New York
Choisy-metric
Contact print on Mylar
12 x 12 inches (30 x 30 cm.)
(Delineator: Michael Barclay)

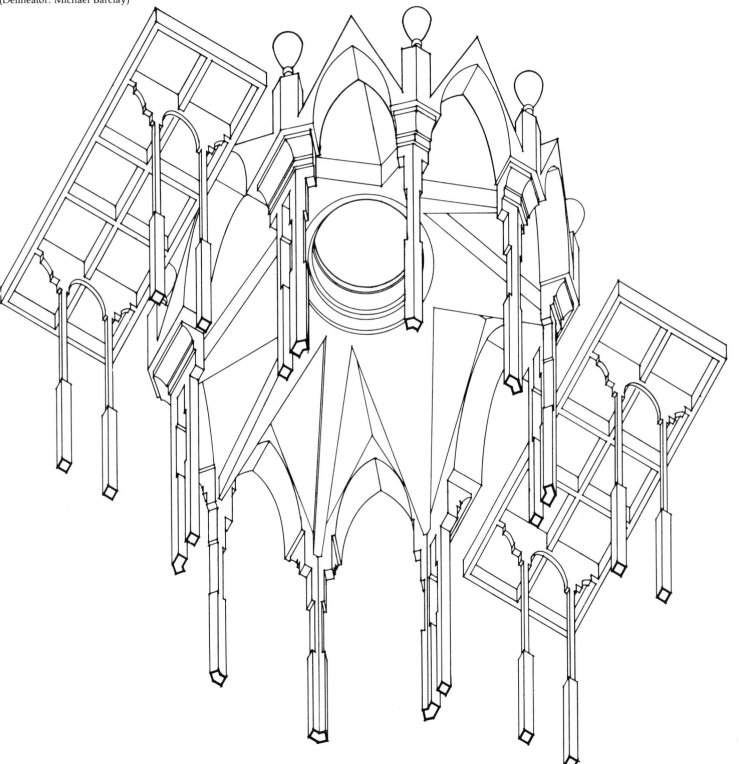

GERALD ALLEN

Cherry Hill Concourse renovation,
Central Park, New York
Perspective
Contact print on Mylar
10 x 17 inches (25 x 43 cm.)
(Delineator: Michael Barclay)

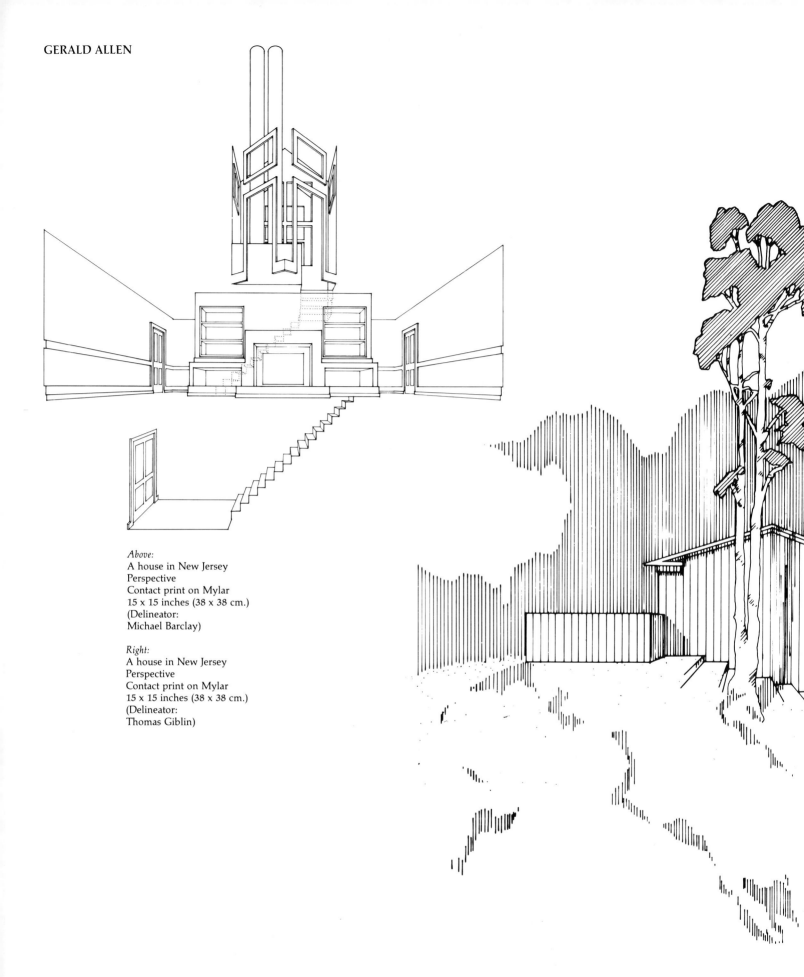

Above:
A house in New Jersey
Perspective
Contact print on Mylar
15 x 15 inches (38 x 38 cm.)
(Delineator:
Michael Barclay)

Right:
A house in New Jersey
Perspective
Contact print on Mylar
15 x 15 inches (38 x 38 cm.)
(Delineator:
Thomas Giblin)

STEVEN K. PETERSON AND BARBARA LITTENBERG

A "finished" drawing is both the end of one process and the beginning of another. It ends the struggle to understand general intentions by making them emerge in illusionary space. The drawing becomes the first full commitment to the thing—an attempt to see the work. It is not just a rendering of what is already known: the production of the drawing itself constitutes design. It requires elaboration, revisions, erasures, and side sketches to complete it. As soon as the drawing is done, however, it begins a process of criticism that must relate back to the conception of the work itself. To do so the drawing must be imagined as habitable, suggesting light, scale, and three-dimensional space. Its value lies not in its own abstract, compositional attributes but in its ability to convey information. As soon as the drawing is completed, it needs to be changed.

Large-scale urban projects, as illustrated here, require representation at both the general and the specific level. Axonometrics show the overall conceptual order and allow the imagination equal access to all the different spaces. Eye-level perspectives suggest the experience of particular places imbedded within the general framework.

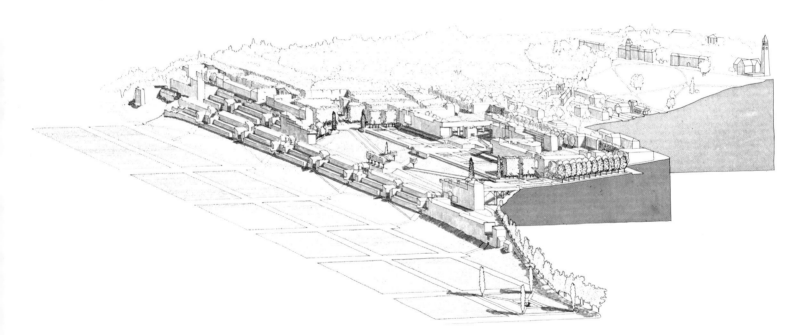

Left:
Project for University Avenue,
Ithaca, New York, 1980
Axonometric: elevation projection
Pencil shadows on photograph of ink on Mylar original
40 x 40 inches (102 x 102 cm.)

Below:
Project for University Avenue,
Ithaca, New York, 1980
Axonometric: plan projection
Pencil shadows on photograph of ink on Mylar original
40 x 40 inches (102 x 102 cm.)

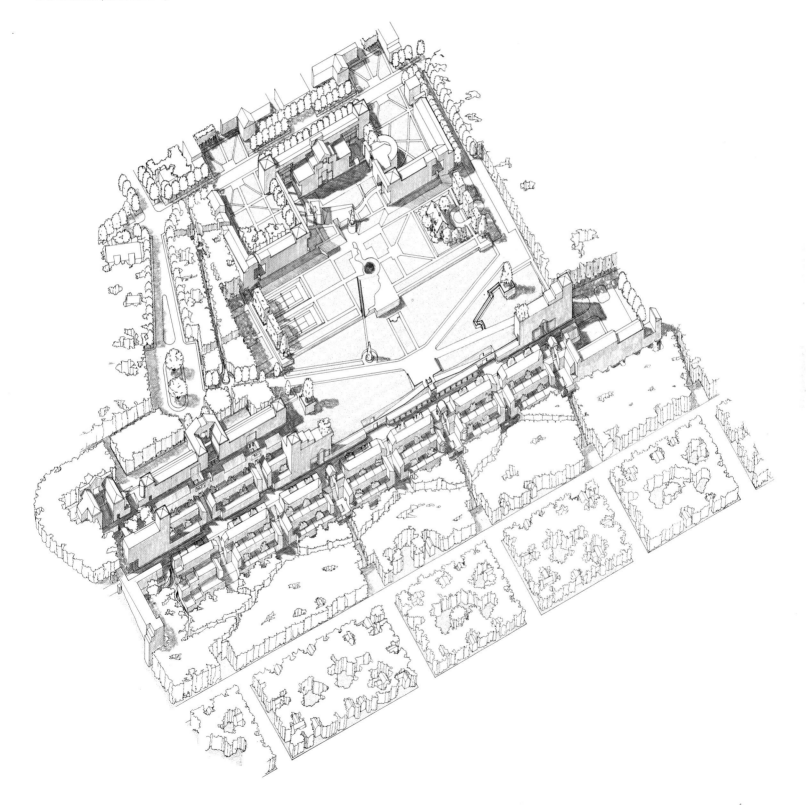

Public Garden,
Project for Les Halles Quarter,
Paris, 1979
Perspective
Oil paint on photograph of ink on Mylar original
22 x 24½ inches (56 x 62 cm.)

Street looking toward St. Eustache,
Project for Les Halles Quarter, Paris, 1979
Perspective
Oil paint on photograph of ink on Mylar original
22 x 24½ inches (56 x 62 cm.)

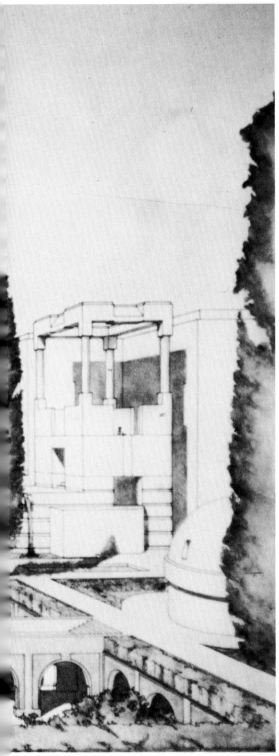

STEFANOS POLYZOIDES

The two sets of axonometric drawings helped us deal with the definition and development of the overall conceptual framework of the house shown here. They classified and resolved the following issues: How does the object meet the ground and the sky? How does the object respond to the assorted scales of the built and landscape context? How does the spatial zoning of the building affect the design of its exterior walls? How is light to become manifest in the building? How can the constructional and structural logic of the building begin to enrich its overall sense? How can the inherent qualities of the building as an environment modifier be made into an integrated part of its architecture? What is the stereometric quality of the object overall, and how does it reflect the *parti* of the building?

Many of these questions had been asked before singly and through the use of other media. But the precision and hardness of the axonometric allowed us to entertain all these questions simultaneously. Axonometrics encourage layered drawing and thinking, and in that sense they can help generate the overall figural qualities of buildings.

The first general task in the design of this house was the distribution of various rooms by type and size relative to vertical and horizontal movement in the building. The axonometrics extended the formal development of the house toward the fixing of its image and its fabric. Perspective drawings followed as the beginnings of the investigation of the nature of places within the house. The emphasis here was not on quality and type of finishes, but rather on the generic qualities of each room, such as the definition of major horizontal and vertical datums and their expression in the design of walls, the proportions of their space, and their connection to other rooms and to the outdoors.

Conversion of UCLA Arroyo Bridge
into a Museum of Cultural Anthropology,
Westwood, California
Perspective
Ink on vellum
36 x 45 inches (91 x 114 cm.)

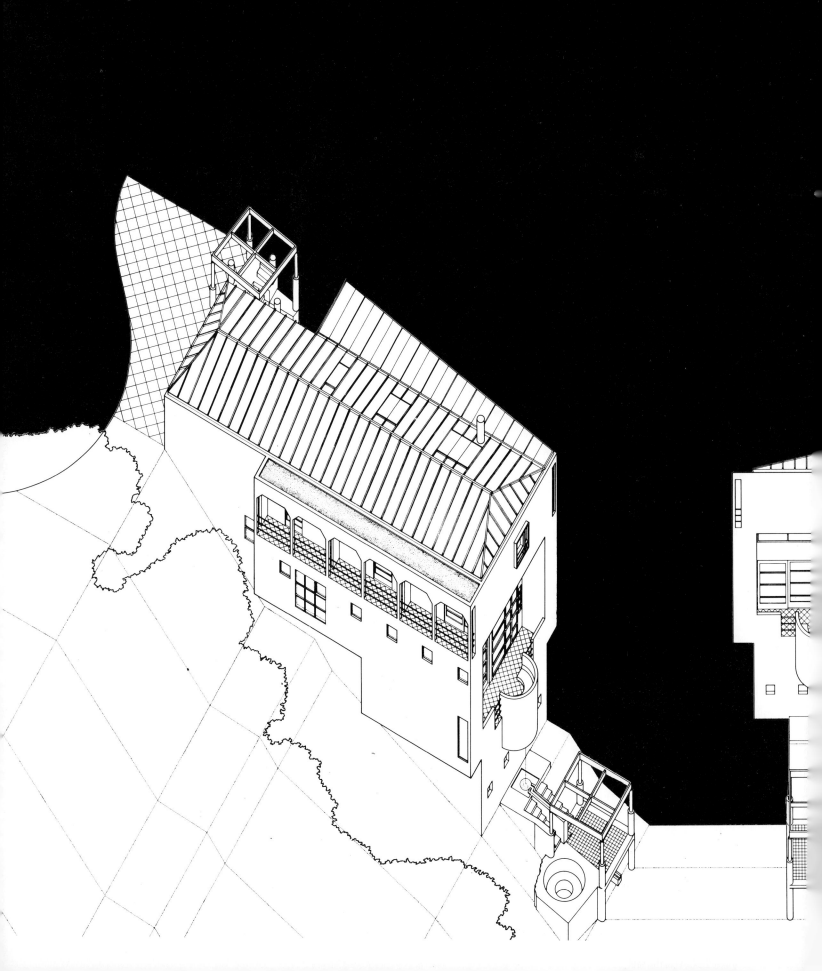

Outer facade, Polyzoides House,
South Pasadena, California
Composite drawing

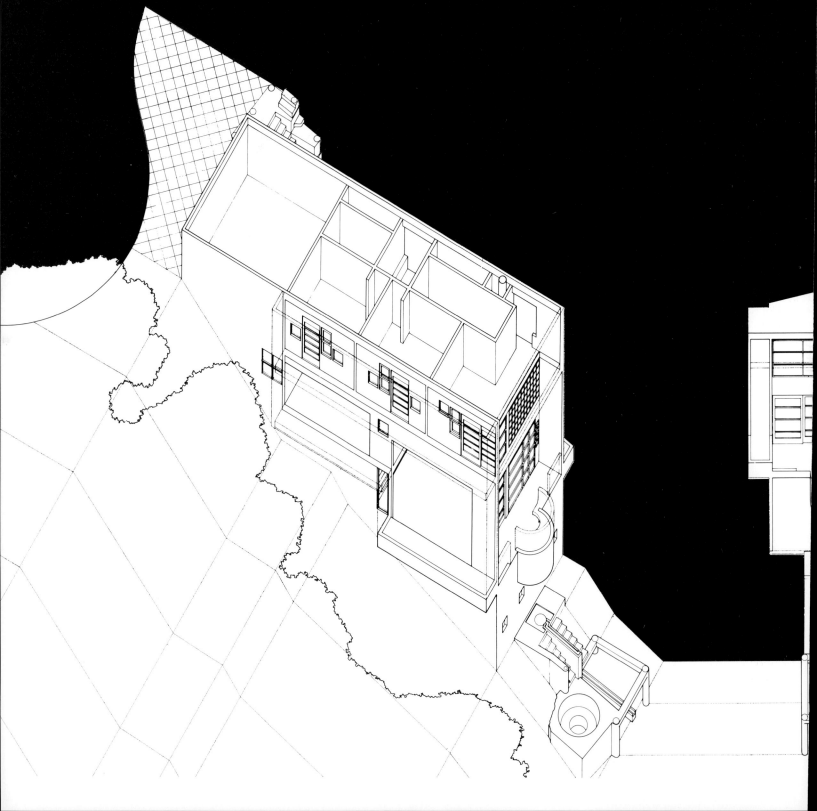

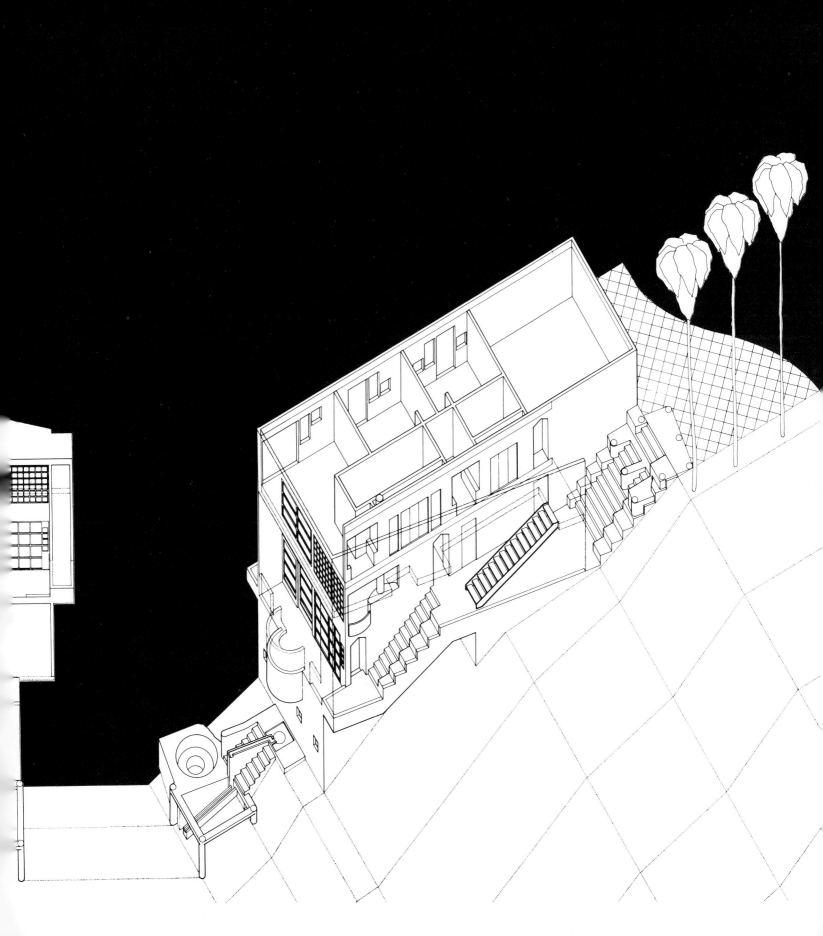

PETER C. PRAN

The axonometric drawing of the Townhouse explains and reveals the entire project: its layering of spaces, entry sequences,
movement patterns, and formal aesthetic
expression. The drawing technique allows
the viewer to relate to the entire design
concept; it is almost transparent.

The bird's-eye view of the Townhouse/
Parking Complex also explains the entire
design concept, and it becomes apparent in
this drawing that the project's wall-like,
contextual character makes a reference to
traditional European urban building ty-
pology. The drawing technique accen-
tuates the project's humane and individ-
ualized solution to urban living and shows
how it breaks new ground in formal and
aesthetic terms.

Traditional interior perspectives are
meaningful to a large number of people,
and they communicate fully the living environment in two townhouses. A refined
ink drawing clearly defines the layering of
the spaces and shows the richly embel-
lished interiors. The exterior perspective is
distorted to give the full impact of the vol-
umetric composition, as well as the juxta-
position of the curved wall surfaces, the
stepped-back roof terrace, and the symbolic entry column. The richness of color
obtainable with the sprayed-ink medium
simulates well the materials: stucco, tile,
glass, and aluminum.

Townhouse, Chicago, Illinois
Axonometric
Ink on Mylar
20 x 16 inches (50 x 41 cm.)

116

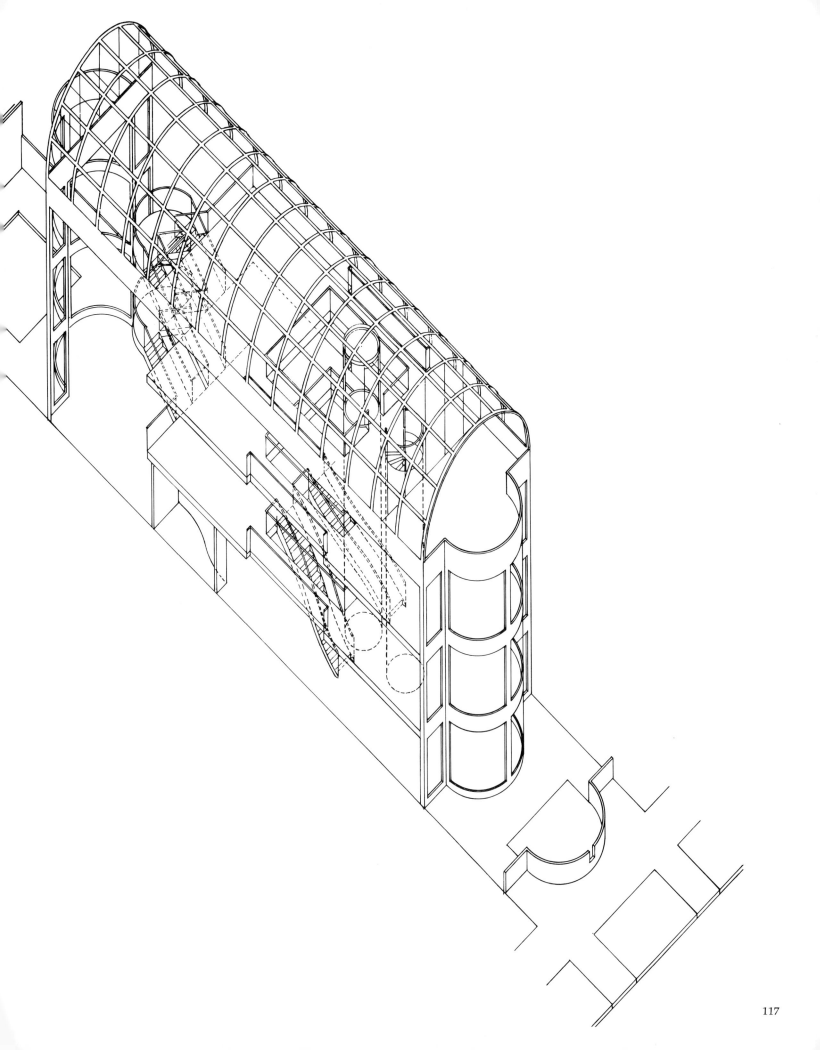

Illinois Institute of Technology
Townhouse/Parking Complex,
Chicago, Illinois
Perspectives
Ink on textured bromide paper
15 x 23 inches (38 x 58 cm.)
(Delineators: Peter C. Pran and Dennis Mika)

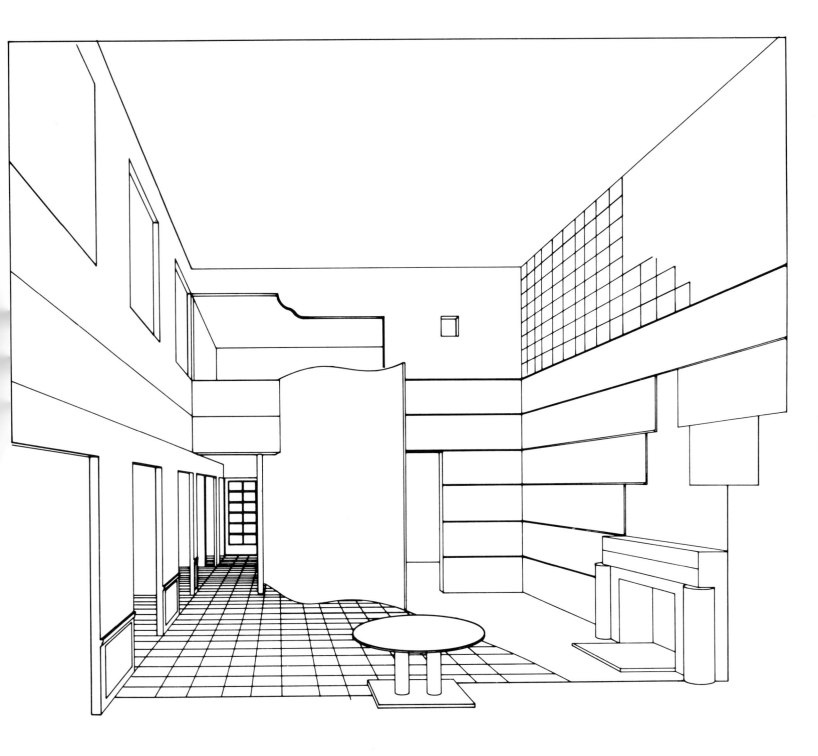

HUGH HARDY, MALCOLM HOLZMAN, AND NORMAN PFEIFFER

The graphic devices are diagrams of enclosure defining the spatial variety that characterizes each building. Areas of black and white are juxtaposed with the gray of newsprint and dot screens to encourage the viewer to consider these drawings as abstract representations rather than literal descriptions. The highly patterned results are consistent with the character of the architecture they define and reflect each structure's inherent organization.

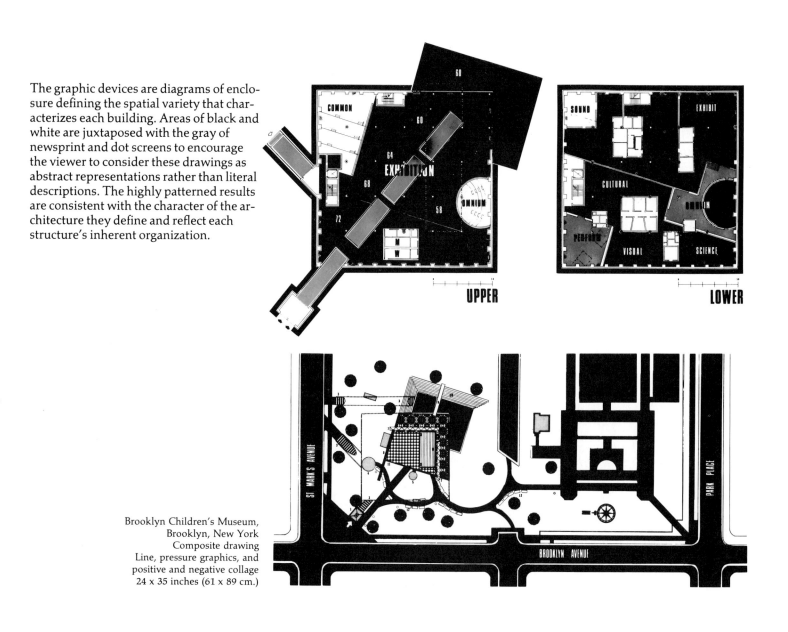

UPPER

LOWER

Brooklyn Children's Museum,
Brooklyn, New York
Composite drawing
Line, pressure graphics, and
positive and negative collage
24 x 35 inches (61 x 89 cm.)

St. Louis Art Museum, St. Louis, Missouri
Composite drawing
Line, pressure graphics, newsprint, photographs,
and positive and negative photographic collage
24 x 20½ inches (61 x 52 cm.)

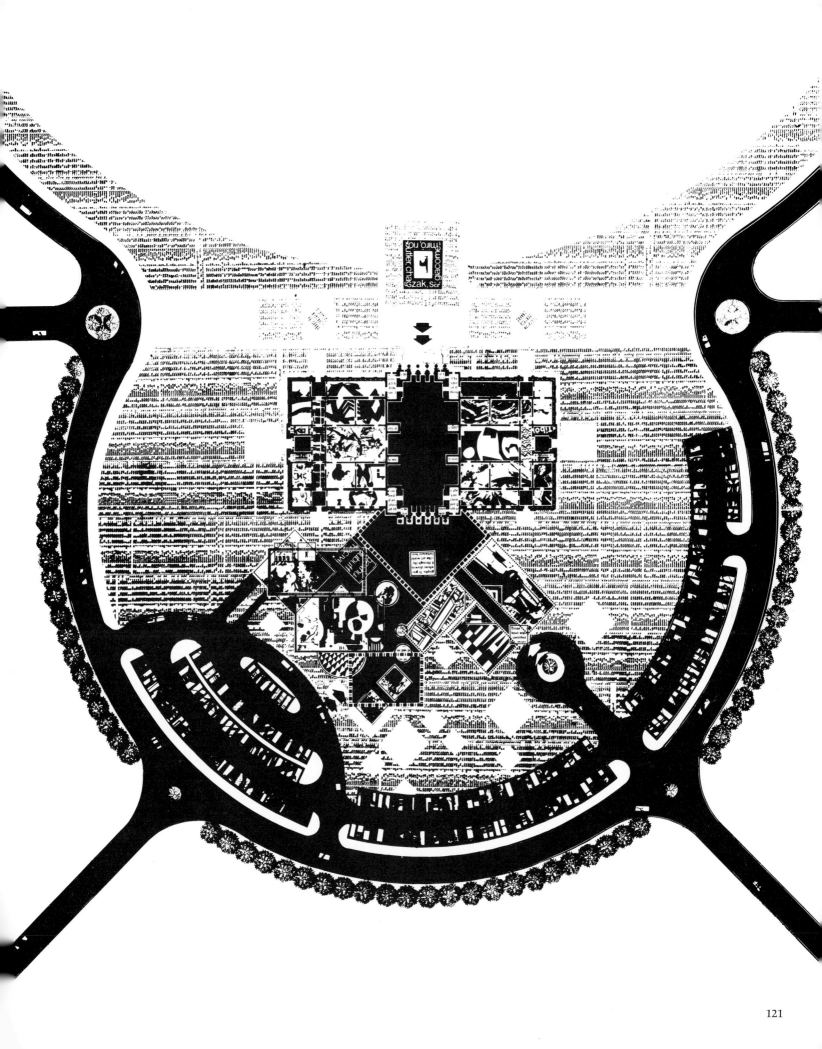

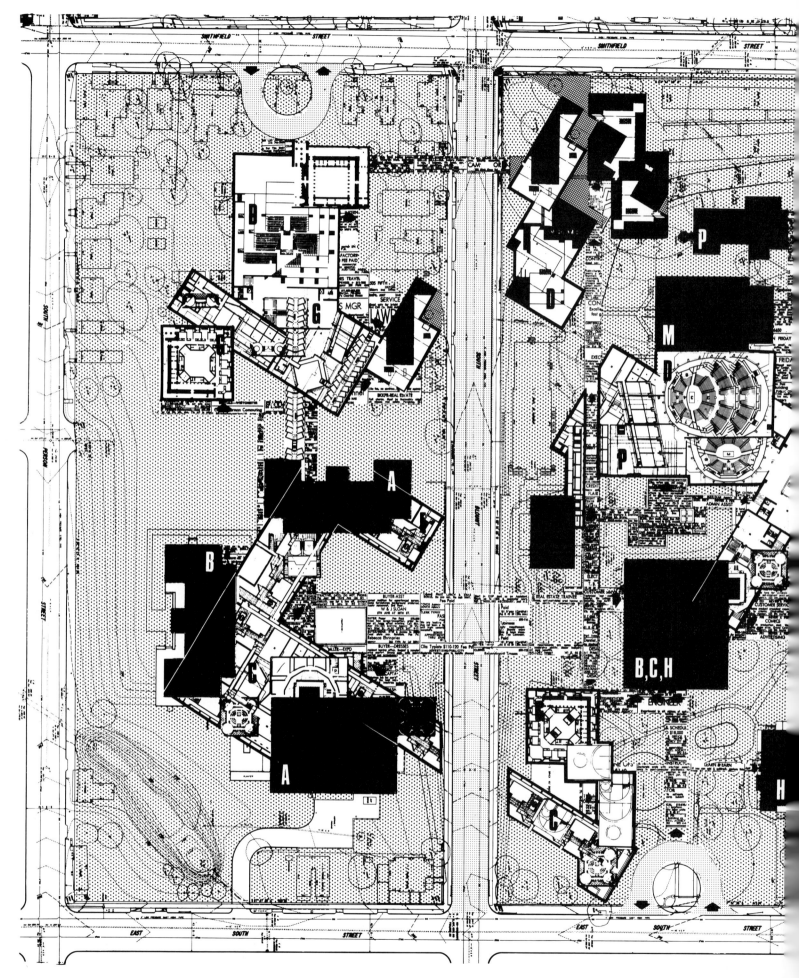

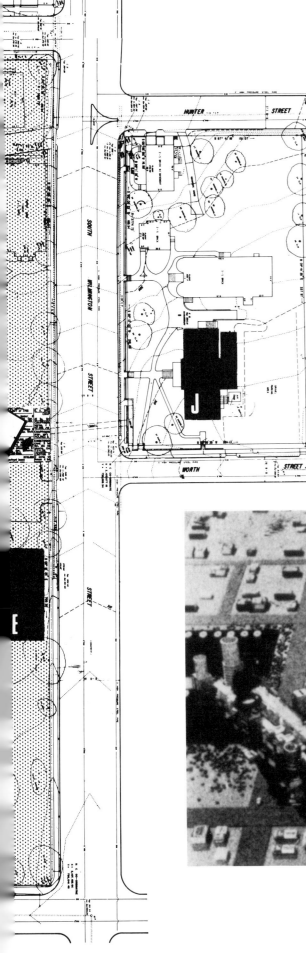

Shaw University, Raleigh, North Carolina
Composite drawing
Line, pressure graphics, newsprint,
topographic map, photograph, and
positive and negative collage
24 x 35 inches (61 x 89 cm.)

MARK MACK

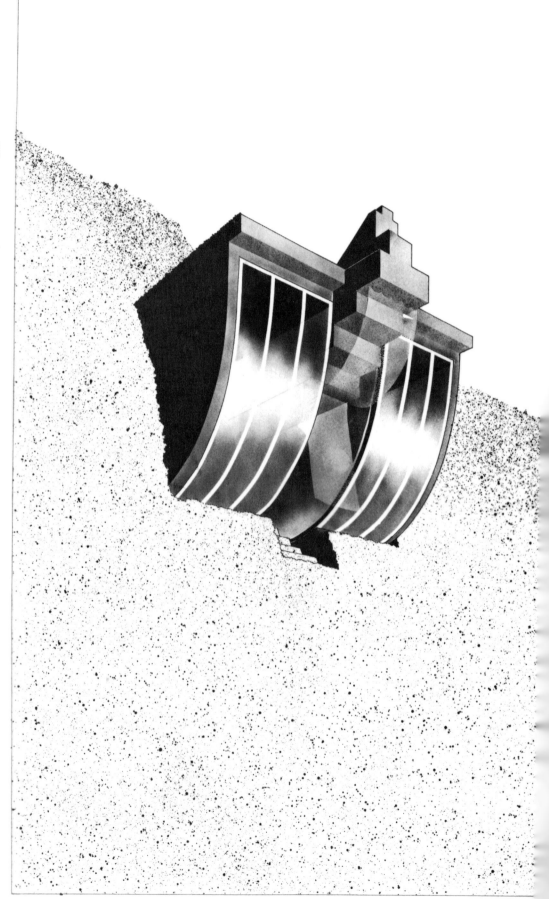

The series of conceptual drawings examines the relationship between man-made form and "god-made" nature. These projects' inspiration is taken from the social, cultural, and ecological concerns prevalent in the northern Californian landscape of the late 1970s. While the buildings are highly functional within their own perimeter, they are all custom designed to fit the particulars of their surroundings. Their intended reading should be amorphous and typological.

While the projects are intended to be real places, their realization is not essential to convey the idea. The drawing technique and the composition of redundant elements in axonometric, plan, section, and interior perspectives, as well as the literal description, contribute to the reading of the drawing as a reality. The airbrush technique employed in the axonometric reinforces this aspect of reality while still being grounded in an abstract and compositional treatment. Only traditional black ink is used in the drawings, even though sometimes blown through an airbrush. The usually slick image of the airbrush technique is eradicated by the stipple effect, a technique usually only achieved by other primitive methods, like blowing through a tube or scraping a toothbrush over wire mesh.

These drawings set the foundations for my new use of the airbrush technique in architectural renderings. Only used as a background and a material suggestion, the technique extends the ideas inherent in the drawings and becomes a carrier of additional information. While my previous attempts dealt with the fascination of the technique itself and its connotations of sleekness and finishedness, this newly found primitive method leads toward a suggestive, analogical, and anthropomorphic imagery, to a familiar abstraction rather than an unfamiliar reality.

Convertible hillside homes
Composite drawing
Airbrushed ink on tracing paper
19½ x 28½ inches (50 x 72 cm.)

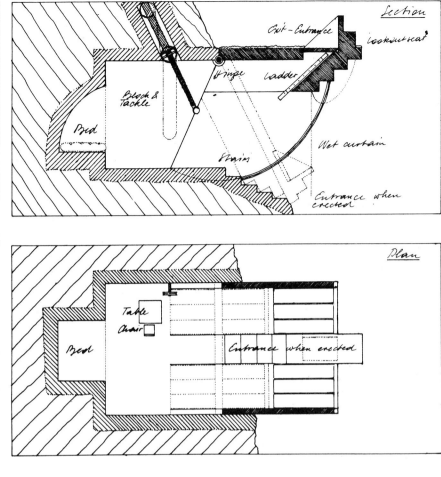

Section

Exit-Entrance

lookout-seat

Hinge

Ladder

Block & Tackle

Bed

Stairs

Wet curtain

Entrance when erected

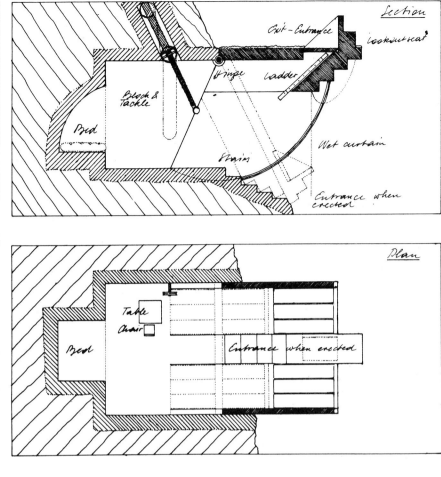

Plan

Table

Chair

Bed

Entrance when erected

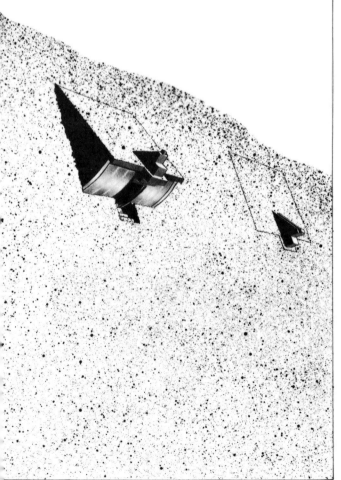

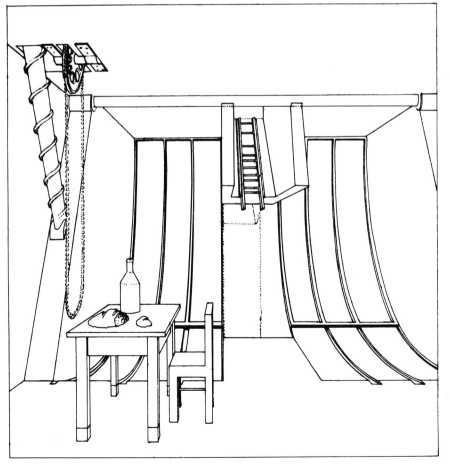

House with a view on a lake
Composite drawing
Airbrushed ink on tracing paper
19½ x 28½ inches (50 x 72 cm.)

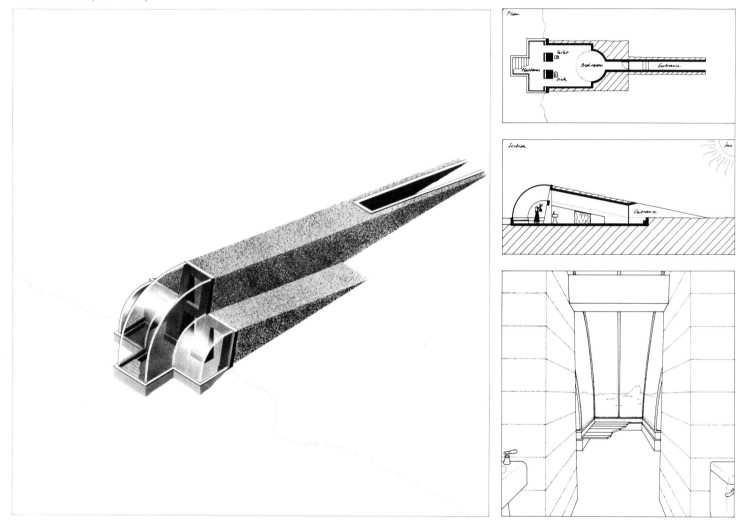

House for two fighting brothers
Composite drawing
Airbrushed ink on tracing paper
19½ x 28½ inches (50 x 72 cm.)

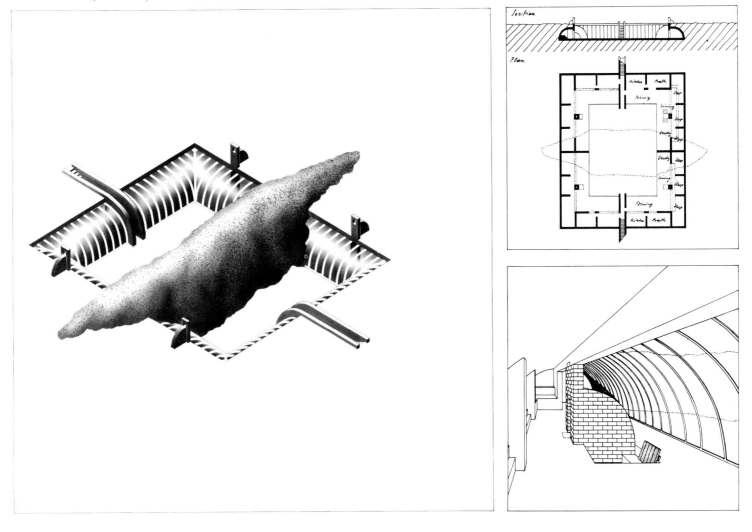

House on the country road
Composite drawing
Airbrushed ink on tracing paper
19½ x 28½ inches (50 x 72 cm.)

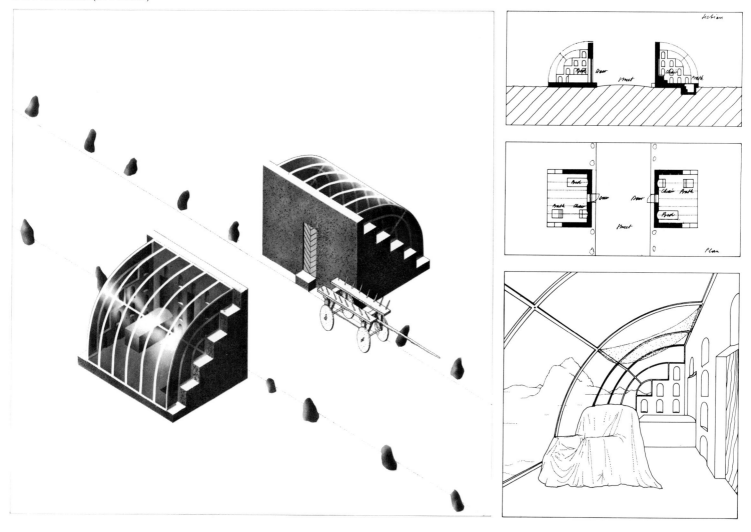

House under ground
Composite drawing
Airbrushed ink on tracing paper
19½ x 28½ inches (50 x 72 cm.)

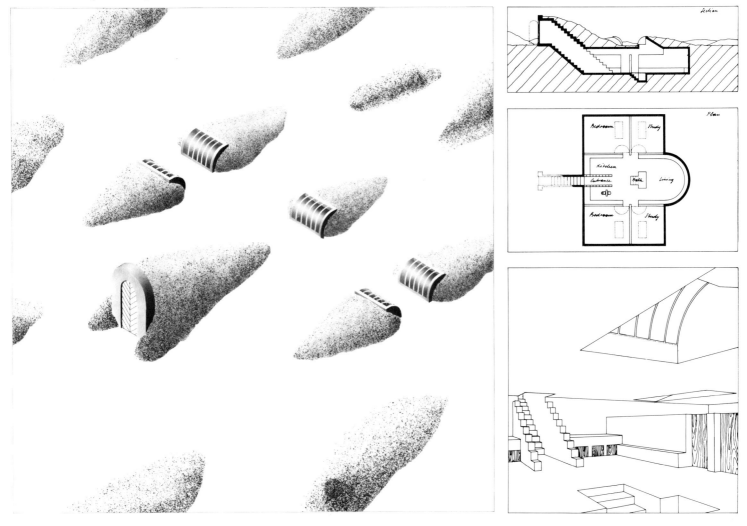

Recreational vehicles camouflaged
Composite drawing
Airbrushed ink on tracing paper
19½ x 28½ inches (50 x 72 cm.)

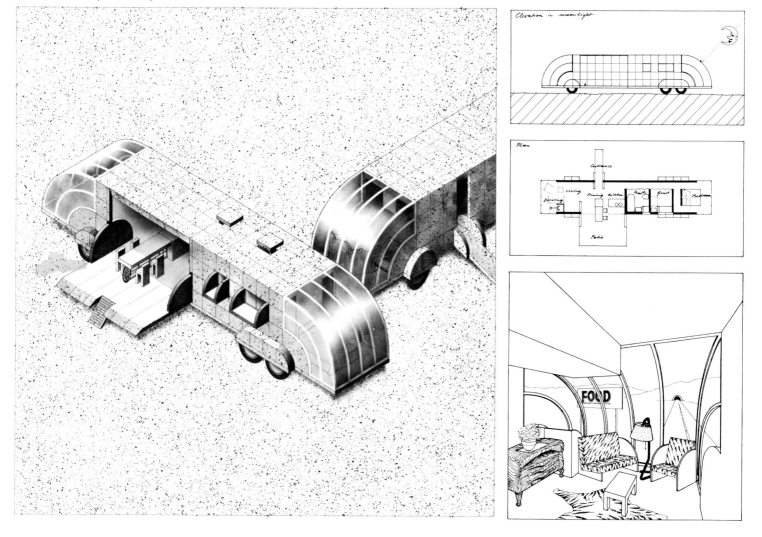

House under a river
Composite drawing
Airbrushed ink on tracing paper
19½ x 28½ inches (50 x 72 cm.)

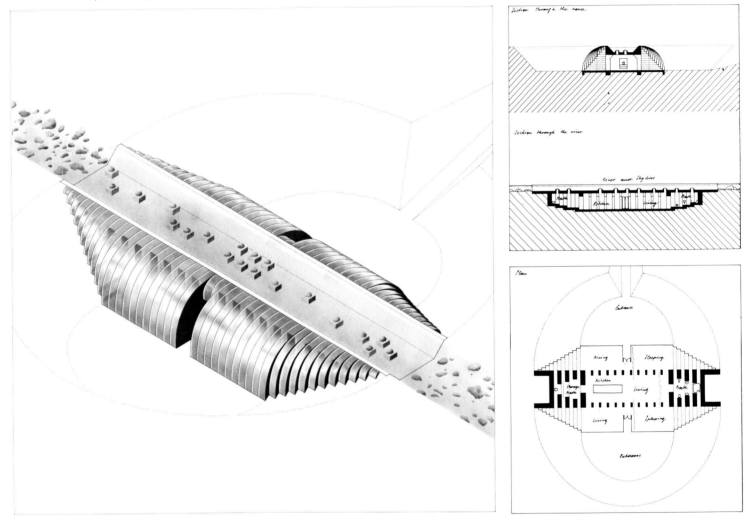

Retreat for mountain climbers
Composite drawing
Airbrushed ink on tracing paper
19½ x 28½ inches (50 x 72 cm.)

Condominiums for high divers and surfers
Composite drawing
Airbrushed ink on tracing paper
19½ x 28½ inches (50 x 72 cm.)

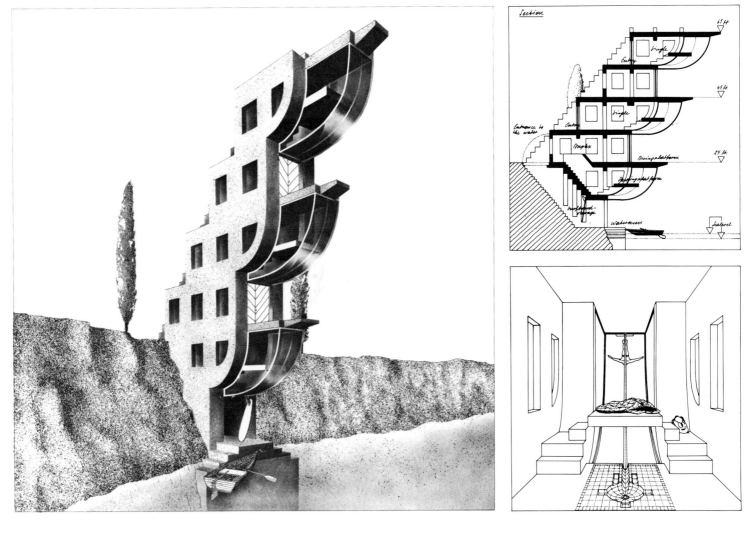

R. M. KLIMENT AND FRANCES HALSBAND

The drawings illustrate our work at three scales: first, the relation of a town to the landscape; second, the relation of an individual building to its immediate surroundings; and third, the relation of detail elements within a single structure. In our work we strive for clarity of organization and richness of visual and tactile experience appropriate to each scale. We seek clarity through hierarchical organization of elements and adjustment of the general organization and particular constraints and by varying the intensity and complexity of elaboration and ornament as appropriate to each element. Our drawings are studies of the relationship of parts to the whole. The scale of each drawing is chosen to focus on a particular relationship or connection. The method, usually drafting rather than sketching, allows accurate dimensions to be maintained. The medium—ink line at smaller scales, color at larger scales—is clear and reproducible, and it serves the purpose of study and presentation.

The axonometric aerial view of the village center in Margaretville is drawn at the scale of one inch to fifty feet. The choice of scale and technique simplifies peripheral elements and focuses attention on the design of the central area of the town and its relationship to the two rivers. This drawing was made for presentation to the town board and merchants' community.

A country house modeled on the eighteenth-century Wythe House in Williamsburg, Virginia, at the request of the client, is derived from a general classical tradition of housebuilding, made particular to the present time, place, and program. The axonometrics of the house and site are drawn at the scale of one-sixteenth inch to one foot. The drawings were made to study the relationship between elevations and landscape. The scale was chosen so that larger elements of the composition could be seen.

The Science Library combines several collections of books in a new structure that is the functional and symbolic center of a science complex and is shown in the site plan at the scale of one inch to fifty feet. The classical composition of the south elevation maintains institutional and architectural continuity with the surrounding campus. This study drawing at the scale of one-quarter inch to one foot shows small elements in relation to the whole.

The renovation of a city apartment focused on an entry hall. Its new relationship to all the adjacent rooms was studied in plan at the scale of one-quarter inch to one foot. The intricate detail of its walls and doors were studied in an elevation drawing at the scale of one-half inch to one foot.

Main Street and Village Center,
Margaretville, New York
Axonometric
Colored pencil on photographic reduction
of ink on Mylar original
11 x 17 inches (28 x 43 cm.)

Project for a house in the country
Axonometrics
Ink on Mylar
24 x 24 inches (61 x 61 cm.)

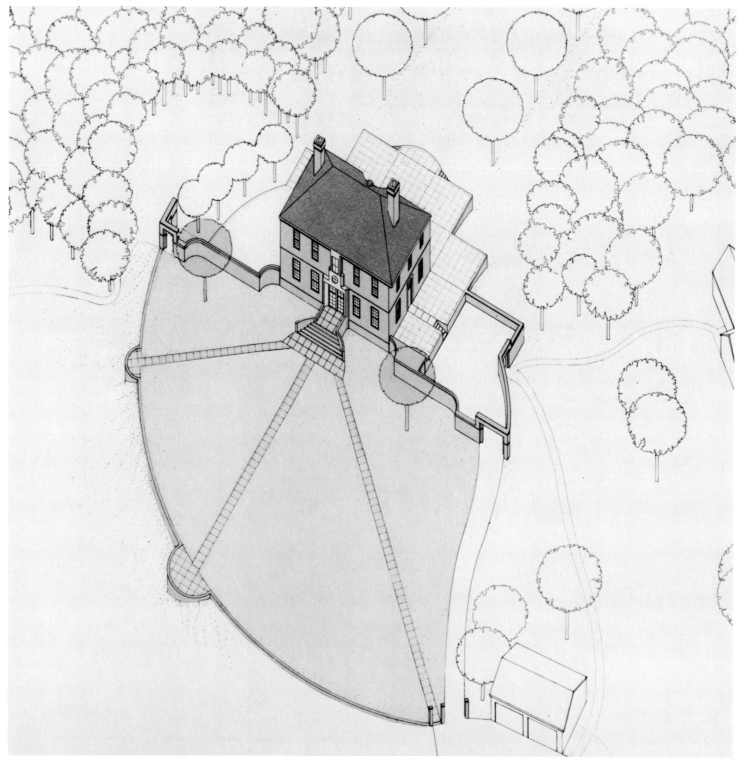

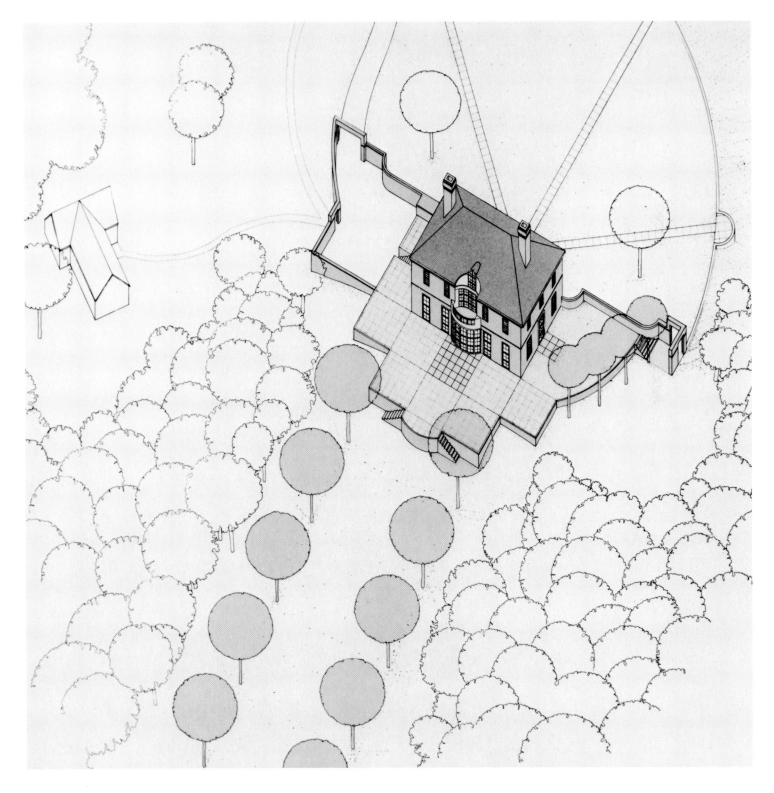

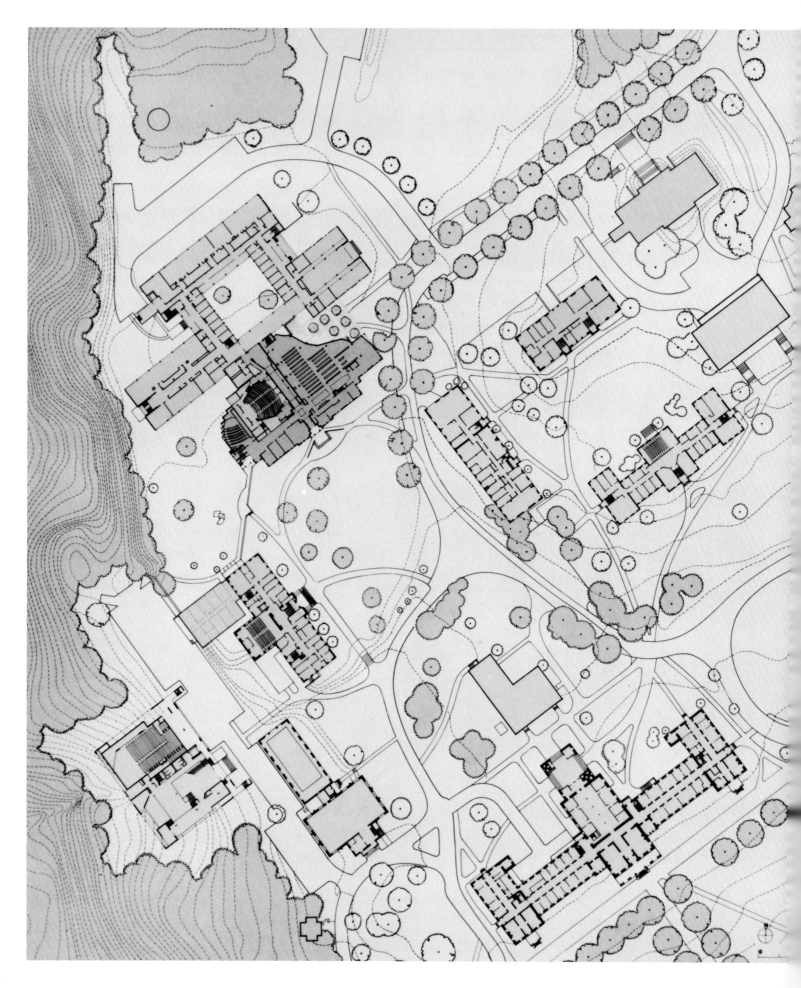

138

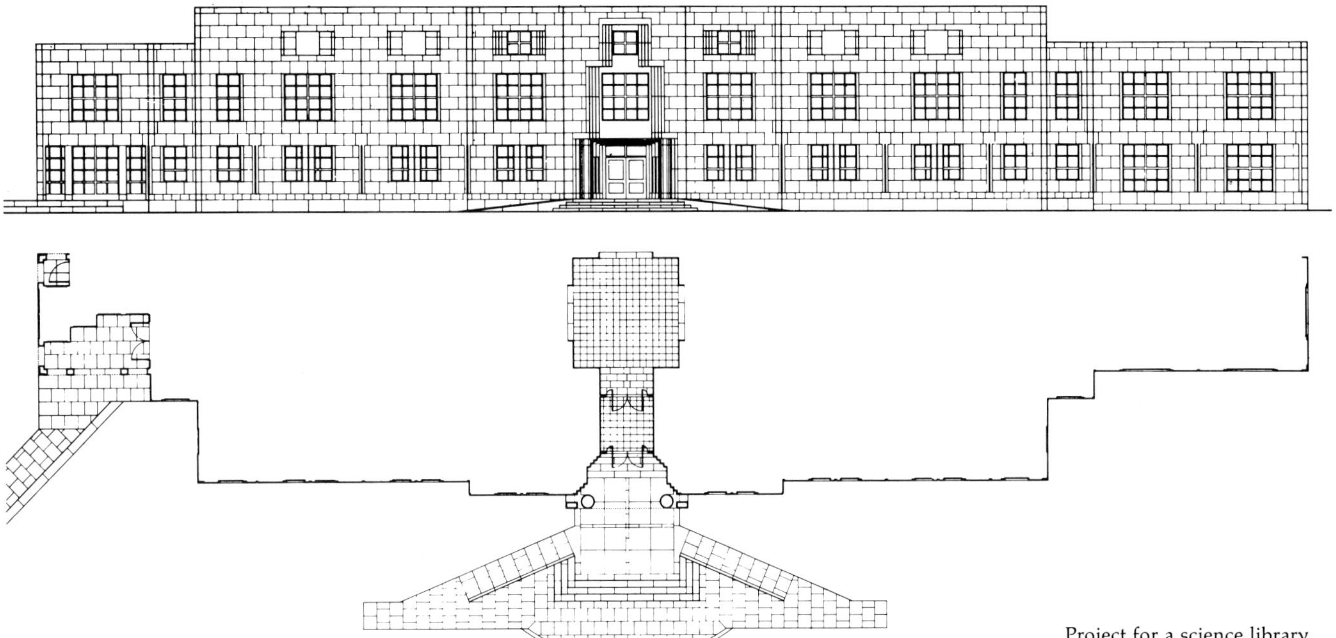

Project for a science library
for Swarthmore College
Elevation
Ink on Mylar
30 x 60 inches (76 x 152 cm.)

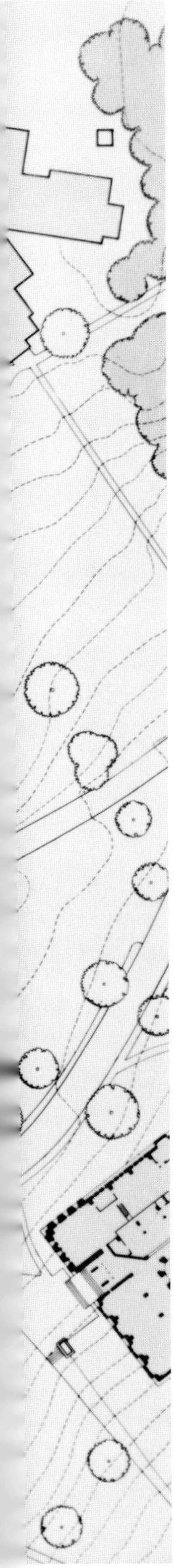

Project for a science library
for Swarthmore College
Site plan
Ink on Mylar
24 x 24 inches (61 x 61 cm.)

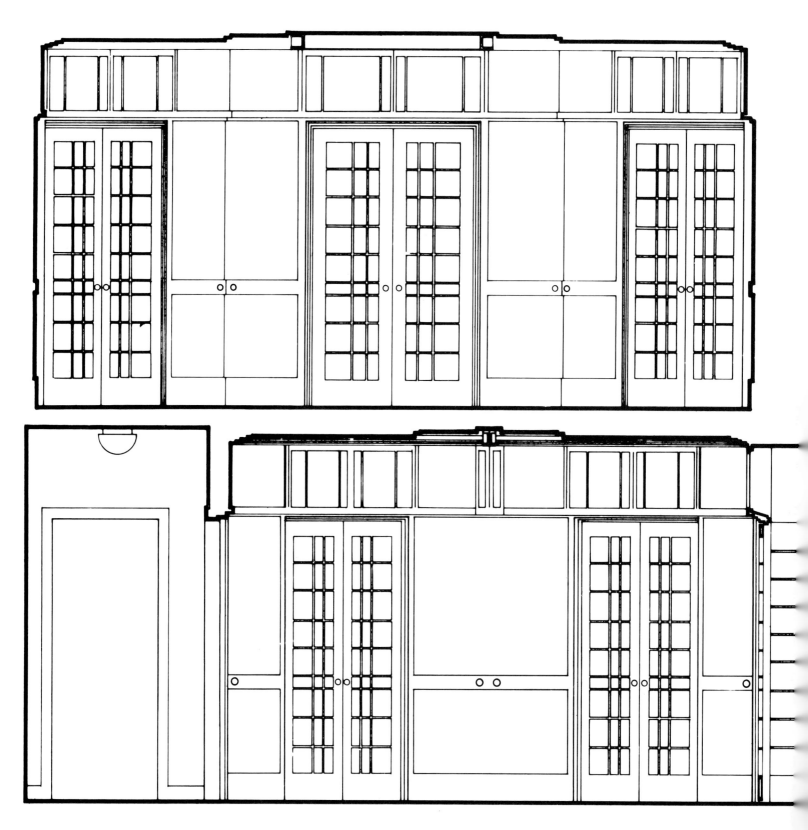

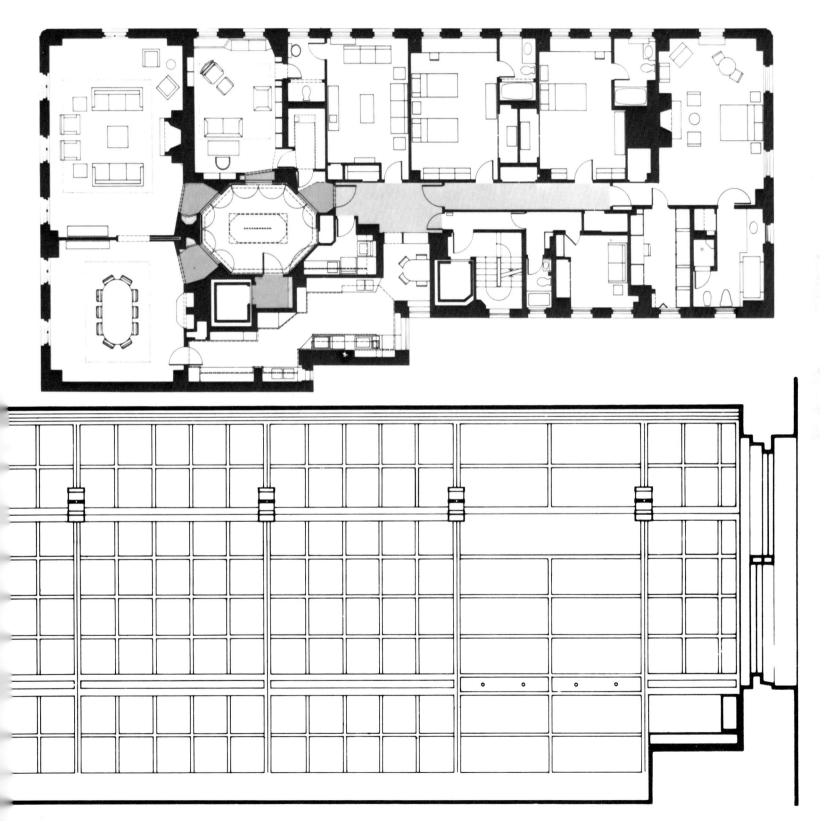

Left:
Apartment, New York City
Elevation
Ink on Mylar
24 x 26 inches (61 x 91 cm.)

Below:
Apartment, New York City
Plan
Ink on Mylar
24 x 36 inches (61 x 91 cm.)

ROBERT VENTURI, JOHN RAUCH, AND DENISE SCOTT-BROWN

The section perspective of the new Children's Zoo at the Philadelphia Zoological Garden is one of a series of section perspectives taken from the entrance to the end of the exhibit. The building is the original Antelope House designed by George W. Hewitt, an early partner of Frank Furness. Given the high Victorian, ecclesiastical plan and section, the section perspective dramatizes the "nave," with its flanking "side chapels," culminating in the Ficus tree "altar." The drawing style has the rich detail and happy sunlit colors of a Victorian children's book illustration.

The elevation studies of the Butler College Dining Hall at Princeton University are two from a series of at least a hundred drawings of the same elevation done over a three- to four-month period. This kind of sketch is for our own edification in developing and refining the elevation. No one drawing tells the story, and one or two elements are altered in each. In these two you can see that the entrance has been moved and combined differently with the vertical windows in order to deal with the difficult formal problem of making an entrance in a long elevation.

The Pylon rendering for the Pennsylvania Avenue Development Corporation shows the ill-fated pylons for the Western Plaza, which fell victim to the aesthetic timidity of Washington, D.C. Their role in the design was that of large-scale, baroque framing elements. The simple, white marble side with its black onyx pinstripe faced the monumental axis of Pennsylvania Avenue. The close-up view from the plaza itself was that of the incised polychrome stars. We gave the drawing a third dimension by making the pylons out of Strathmore Board and cutting out the stars and words. The edge elevation was almost minimalist in its thinness and with its yellow polychrome stripe.

The entrance perspective of the New Capitol of Australia Competition is a good example of a very simple, almost minimal profile drawing done with outline but very little texture or shading. It is a drawing style that depends on evocative profiles of representational objects, perfect selection of view, and elegant cropping to imply the detail that is not drawn. In this drawing, the major challenge was to give a sense of the monumental, curving entrance front and wall in contrast to the small-scale elements of the seal, cars, and people.

The photomontage of Hennepin Avenue illustrates a preliminary idea for the design of a decorative lighting scheme for the entertainment district in Minneapolis, Minnesota. By reverse printing, a positive, daytime color slide was turned into a night view with the addition of an overlay of gray Pantone. The decorative lighting effect—"sparkle trees"—was added with colored paper. The use of a photomontage in dealing with a "Main Street" design problem reflects our predilection not to alter radically the existing street but rather, by adding some carefully considered elements, to improve what's already there.

The drawing of Washington Avenue represents a final presentation rendering for an urban design project. The original pencil line perspective is taken from an enlargement of a slide photographed from a car driving along the avenue. The new palm tree, flowering plants, striped awnings, and lamps that are part of the design solution are added in outline. The drawing is then photographed and printed on KC-5 paper. The pastel colors for the buildings and bright stripes for the awnings that were recommended in the study and a Miami blue sky are overlayed on the line print with Pantone color film.

THE NE

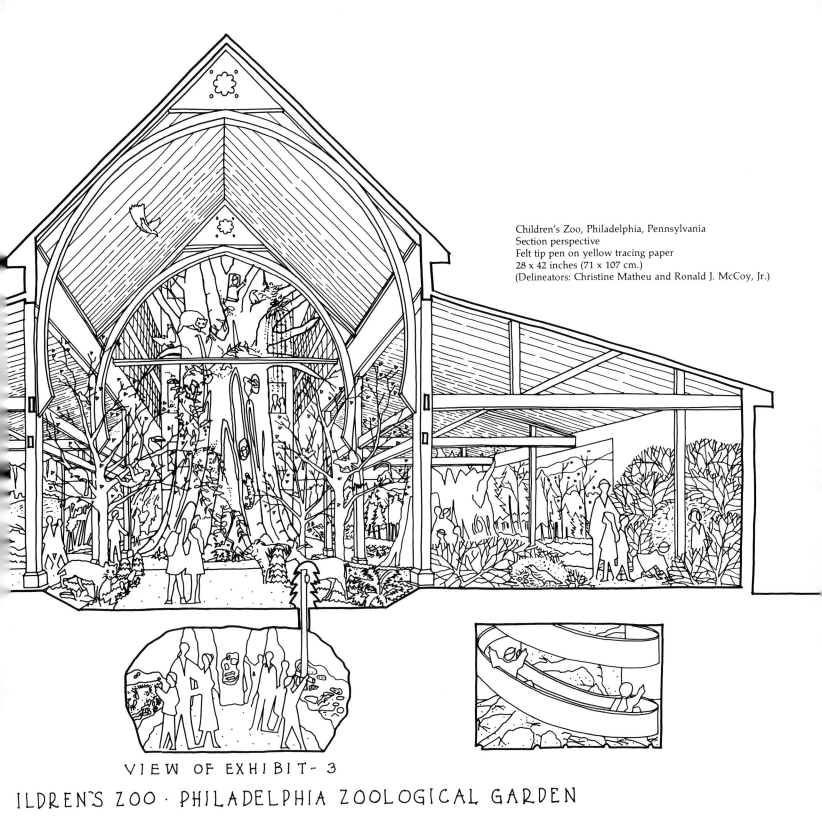

Children's Zoo, Philadelphia, Pennsylvania
Section perspective
Felt tip pen on yellow tracing paper
28 x 42 inches (71 x 107 cm.)
(Delineators: Christine Matheu and Ronald J. McCoy, Jr.)

VIEW OF EXHIBIT- 3

ILDREN'S ZOO · PHILADELPHIA ZOOLOGICAL GARDEN

FEBRUARY 20, 1981
VENTURI , RAUCH AND SCOTT BROWN

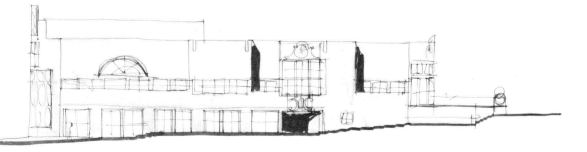

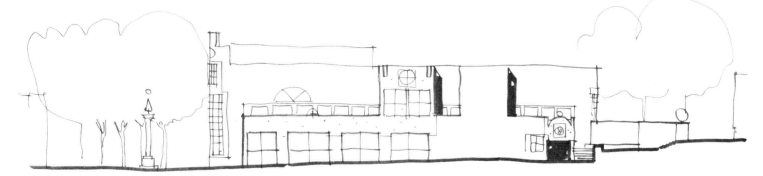

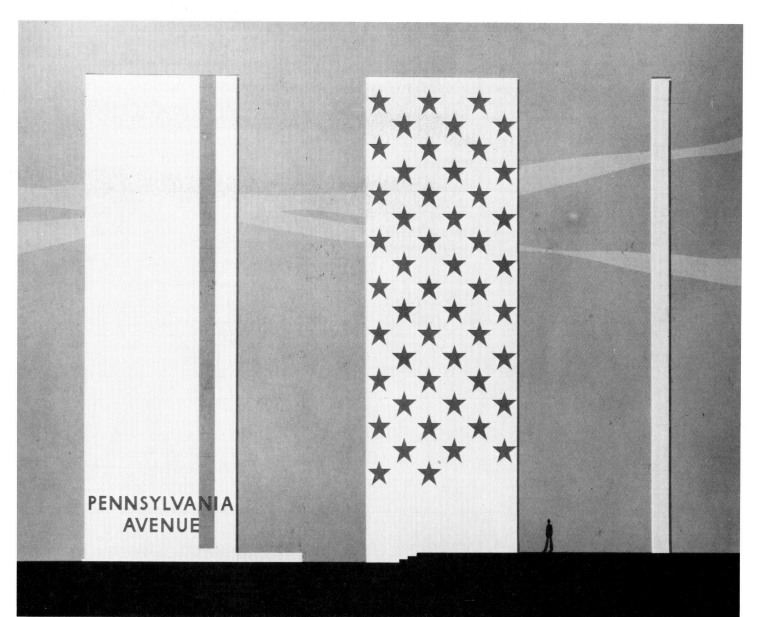

PENNSYLVANIA
AVENUE

Capitol of Australia, Canberra
Perspective
KC-5 print with Pantone
20 x 40 inches (51 x 102 cm.)

PARLIAMENT HOUSE CANBERRA · 1979

Left above:
Butler College Dining Hall,
Princeton University, Princeton, New Jersey
Elevations
Felt tip pen on yellow tracing paper
with Magic Marker
12 x 30 inches each (30 x 76 cm.)
(Delineator: Robert Venturi)

Left:
Pylon, Pennsylvania Avenue, Washington, D.C.
Elevations
Pencil, cut paper, and Pantone
on Strathmore board
29 x 35 inches (74 x 89 cm.)
(Delineators: Tony Atkin and Steve Izenour)

Hennepin Avenue, Minneapolis, Minnesota
Perspective
Photograph, colored paper, and Pantone
16 x 20 inches (41 x 51 cm.)
(Delineator: James H. Timberlake)

Washington Avenue, Miami Beach, Florida, 1979
Perspective
KC-5 print with Pantone
24 x 36 inches (61 x 91 cm.)
(Delineator: Frederic Schwartz)

GEORGE RANALLI

Chicago Tribune Tower Competition/Late Entries
Perspective
Colored pencil, airbrush, and photomontage
on sepia print paper
60 x 30 inches (152 x 76 cm.)

The types of drawings I use are the orthographic projections of plan, section, and elevation and the oblique projection for the complete view. Each of the orthographic projections explores ideas about the architecture capable only of being studied in that particular view. Plans are drawn as maps of the structure, while the sections and elevations depict the characteristics of space and form. In the sections, there is an attempt to give an atmospheric content to the space, an aroma or a smell. The elevations pursue the density of the mass in relationship to the landscape. The combination of these drawings expresses the structure abstractly, as well as emotionally.

The oblique projection is used to combine the conceptual and perceptual drawing. In the layout, the deliberate choice of the elevation oblique is combined with the elements of the architecture, as well as the landscape, to completely interconnect the idea of drawing to the idea of building. The drawing is then represented with all the phenomena of shade, shadow, and light to allow it to be read perceptually. Also exploited in these views are the issues of materiality, surface, and texture, all of which allow the drawing to convey multiple readings.

The medium of graphite line drawing with colored pencil is used on several drawings, also combined with airbrush and photomontage. Color application with pencils allows for a lengthy process of building up tones by covering the drawing with many layers of color. This process permits subtle color changes across the surface of the building, which attempts to give the feeling of what might be taking place in the structure itself. It is not meant to be a literal representation but a metaphorical relationship, giving the viewer the sensation of the building, not its reality.

Frehley House, Stratford, Connecticut
Section
Prismacolor on paper
10 x 33 inches (25 x 84 cm.)

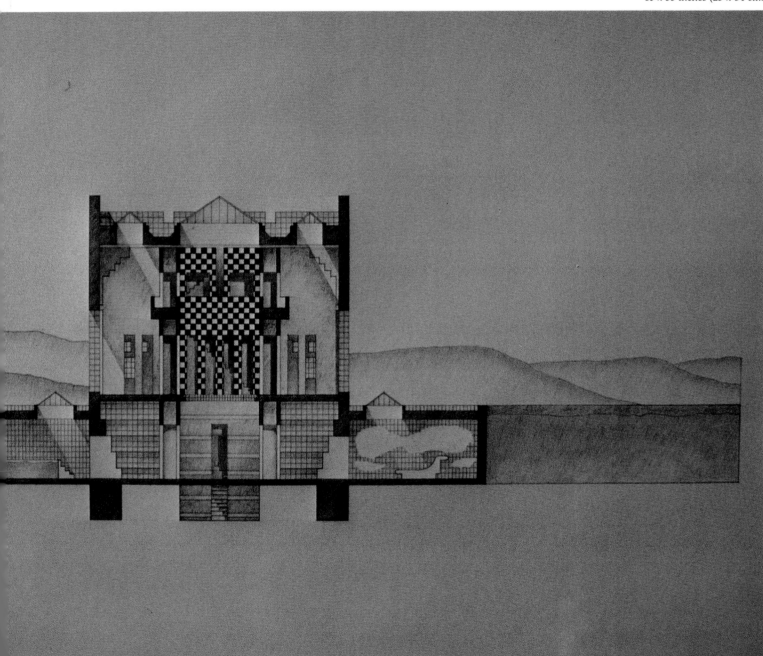

CHARLES MOORE

I don't believe that architectural drawings are either an end in themselves or just an unadorned means to another end, the built building. Rather they constitute a pleasurable dalliance along the way, a heady celebration of the circumstantial. I remember the enormous excitement that came from watching Lou Kahn draw a plan whose columns, ordered according to the most elaborate structural metaphysics, were rendered exactly the same as the tree trunks scattered randomly about the site as though signals were being plotted from some mysterious extraterrestrial source and organized into an almost comprehensible tongue.

For the reasons that follow closely on this excitement, I enjoy easy media—Eagle drafting pencils, Prismacolor, Pilot pens—that let the straightforward recording of possibilities for the building design at hand wander into arrangements I hadn't dreamed of before the pencil slid across the paper. I don't know why, but if the paper is tracing paper, it has to be yellow, preferably bright yellow. The white stuff stops me cold, though white *watercolor* paper is fine. If the black pencil isn't a 314 Eagle, I lapse into sullen unproductivity, but I'll cheerfully switch, and often so, to a Pilot razor-point pen. I don't remember how I managed before they came on the market. I like watercolors too if I can leave the more precise parts to linear doodlers like the Pilot pen.

So for others are the dazzling drawings meant as the product. These are for singing along, or just humming.

A public plaza, Portland, Oregon
Elevation
Colored pencil on yellow tracing paper
12 x 15 inches (30 x 38 cm.)

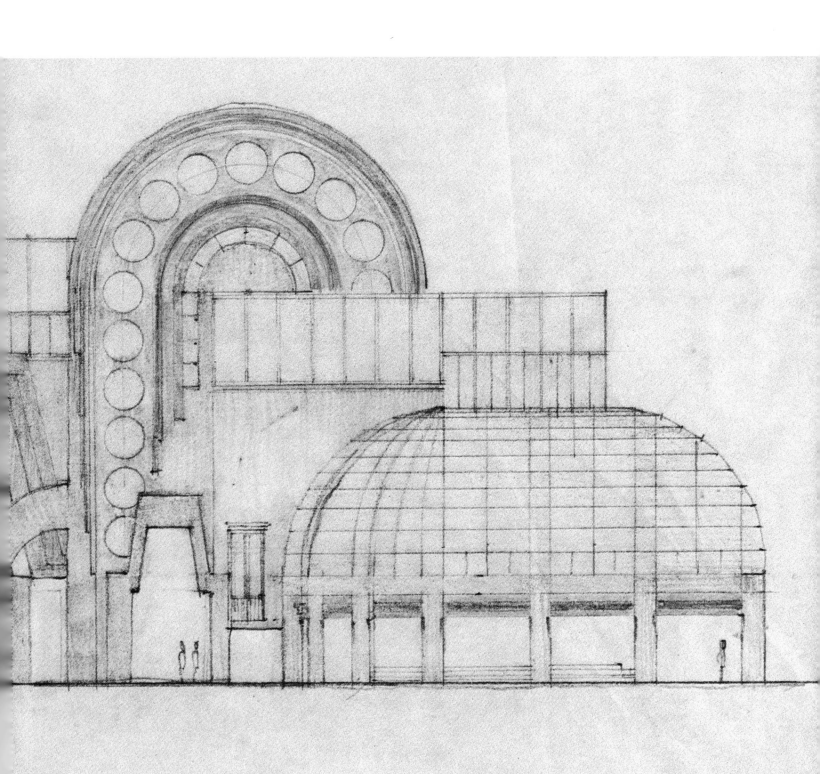

Left and below left:
A public plaza, Portland, Oregon
Elevations
Colored pencil on yellow tracing paper
12 x 15 inches (30 x 38 cm.)

Below:
A public plaza, Portland, Oregon
Plan
Pencil on yellow tracing paper
28 x 24 inches (71 x 60 cm.)

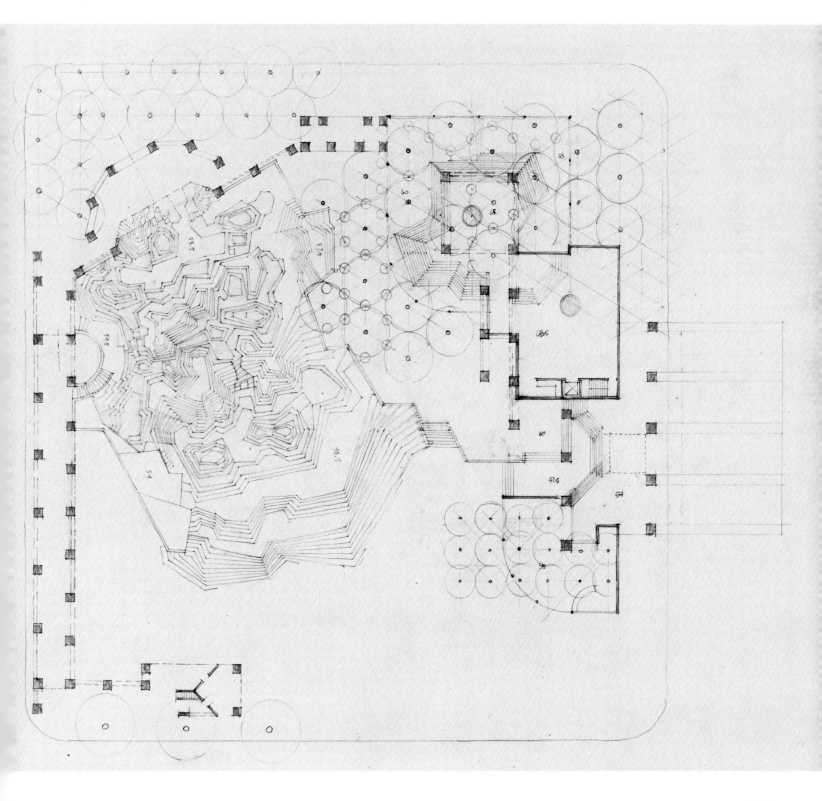

A public plaza, Portland, Oregon
Elevations
Colored pencil on yellow tracing paper
12 x 15 inches (30 x 38 cm.)

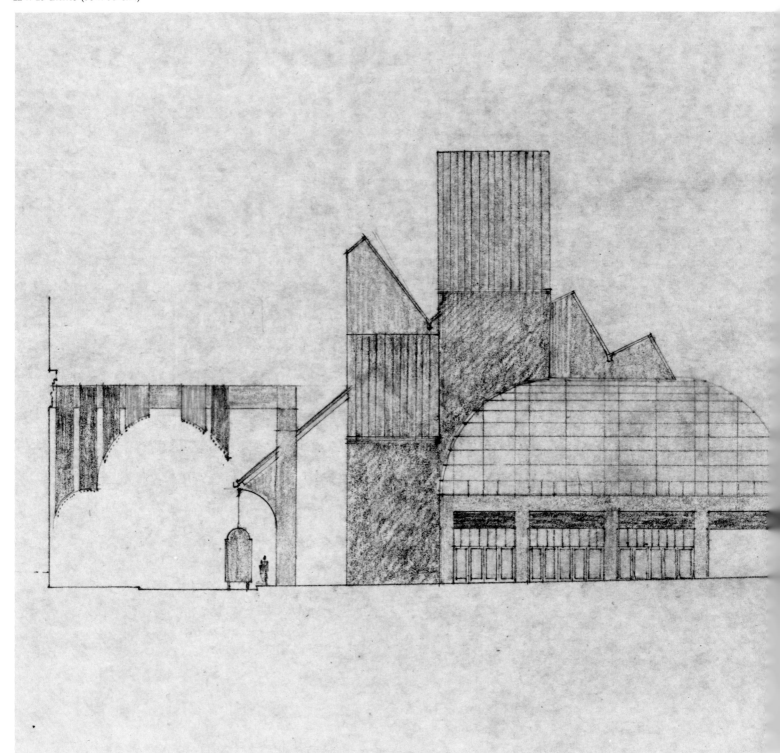

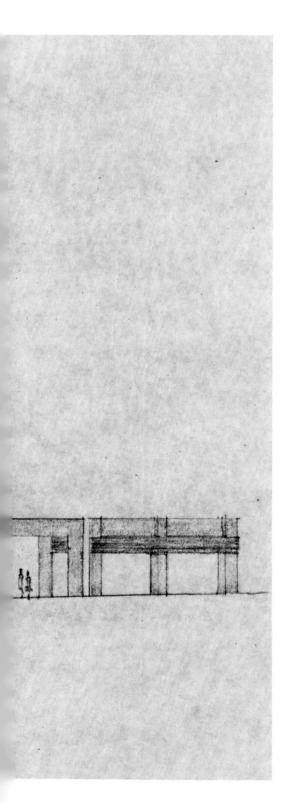

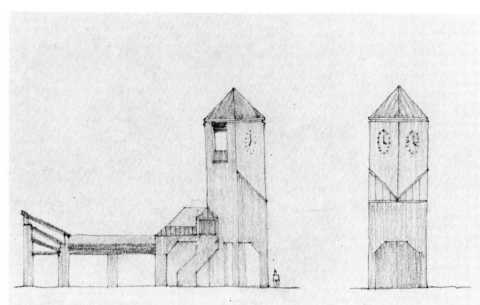

STANLEY TIGERMAN

The drawings are elevation studies of a particular project. In addition to the particularities, the purpose of drawings like these is in general twofold. The first is to communicate from me to myself through multiple images so that they feed back to my own hand, since the drawings an architect makes for himself and the methods he chooses convey to him certain information that is useful. The second is that these same drawings, at least in my own practice, are always shown to the client, since the process of design is one that embraces the client's participation in the development of the design. Little sophistication beyond what the drawing literally represents is required to directly communicate with one's self and with the client.

Another reason for the inclusion of these particular drawings is my growing concern about what is sometimes pejoratively called "extrinsic" in architecture—the making of images, the conveying of information about a building through whatever one sees, and the public facade versus the private plan.

National Archive Center
for the Baha'i Faith in the United States
Perspective
Airbrush on Strathmore board
18 x 24 inches (46 x 61 cm.)

Villa Proeh I
Elevation
Pencil and Prismacolor on yellow tracing paper
12 x 16 inches (30 x 43 cm.)

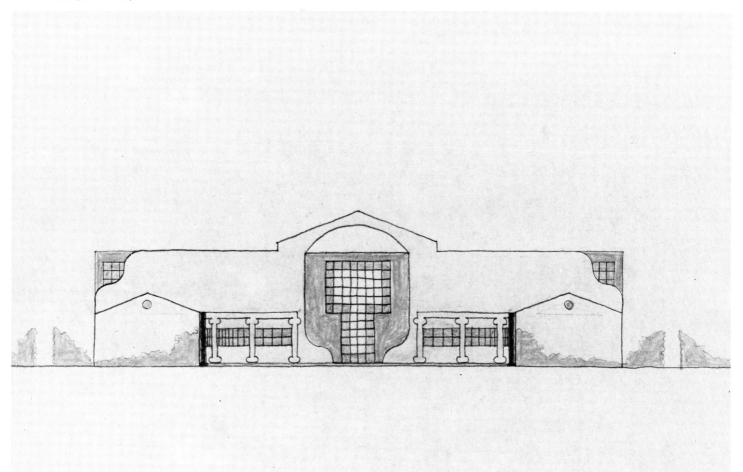

VILLA PROEH I, 1979 Stan Tigerman

Villa Proeh II
Elevation
Pencil and Prismacolor on yellow tracing paper
12 x 14 inches (30 x 43 cm.)

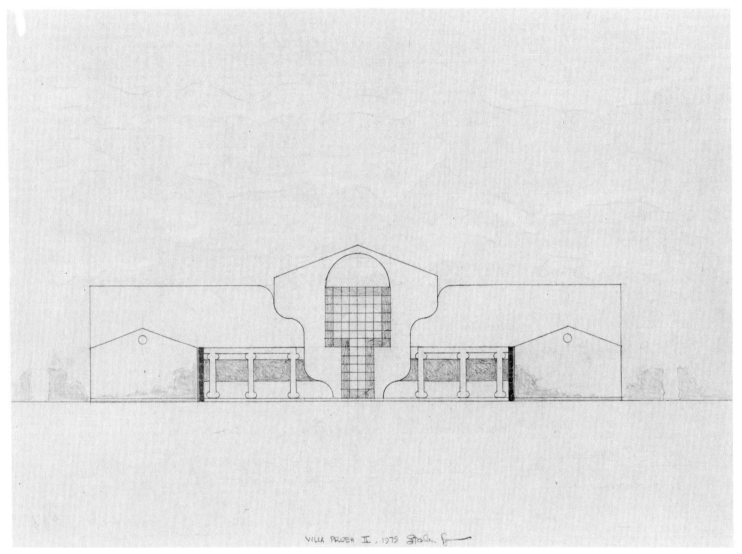

Villa Proeh III
Elevation
Pencil and Prismacolor on yellow tracing paper
12 x 16 inches (30 x 43 cm.)

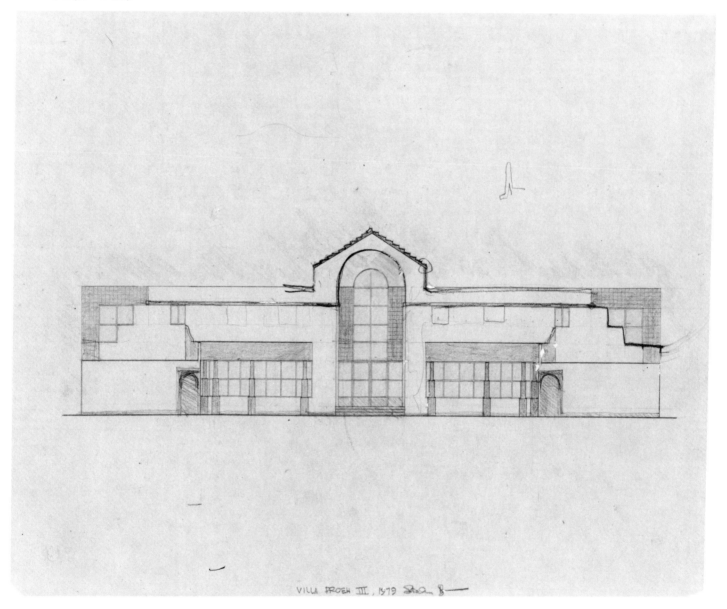

Villa Proeh IV
Elevation
Pencil and Prismacolor on yellow tracing paper
12 x 16 inches (30 x 43 cm.)

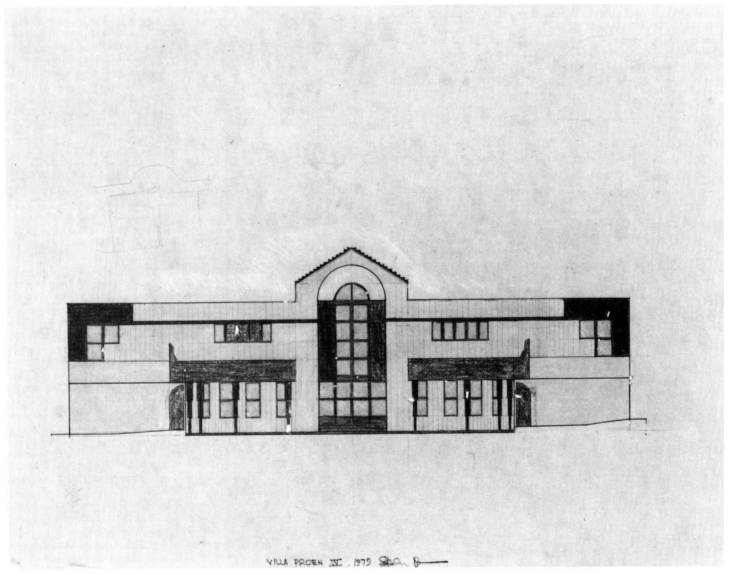

Villa Proeh V
Elevation
Pencil and Prismacolor on yellow tracing paper
12 x 16 inches (30 x 43 cm.)

Villa Proeh VI
Elevation
Pencil and Prismacolor on yellow tracing paper
12 x 16 inches (30 x 43 cm.)

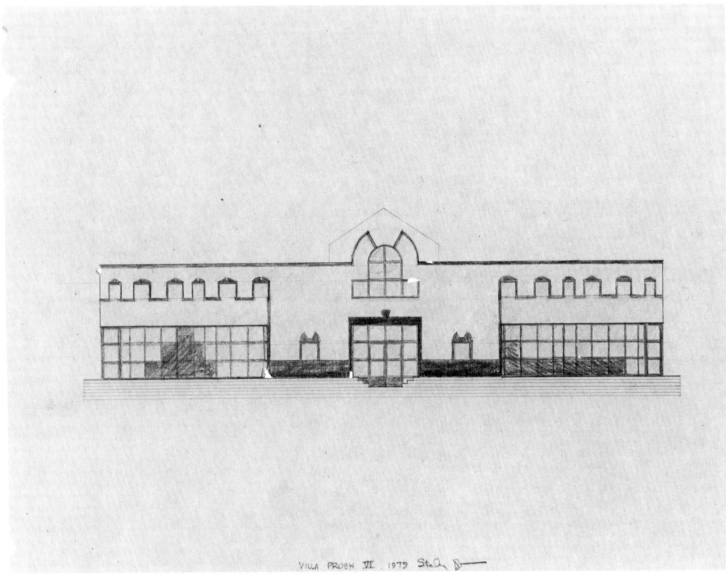

VILLA PROEH VI . 1979 Stan D

Villa Proeh VII
Elevation
Pencil and Prismacolor on yellow tracing paper
12 x 16 inches (30 x 43 cm.)

VILLA PROEH VIII, 1979

Villa Proeh VIII
Elevation
Pencil and Prismacolor on yellow tracing paper
12 x 16 inches (30 x 43 cm.)

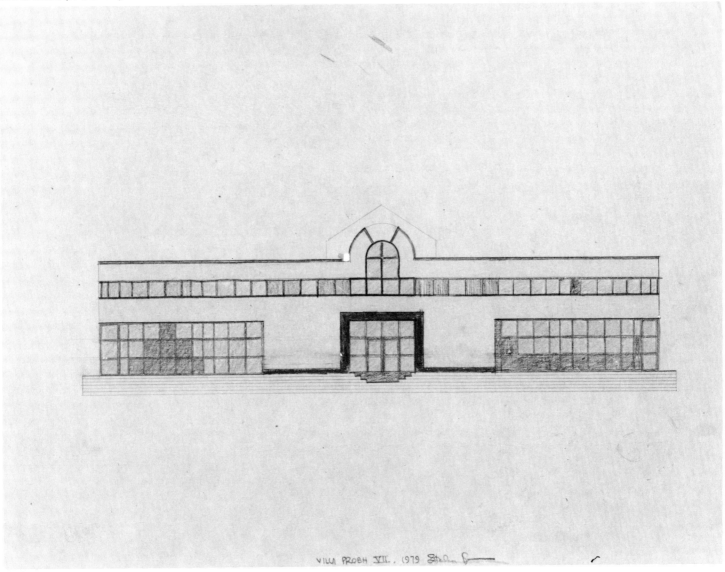

VILLA PROEH VII. 1979

TURNER BROOKS

The drawings make a project palpable and real in a way that line drawings and even models cannot. They are atmospheric visions of a building as I see it—here the image of a ship steaming through the night, lights reflecting off water, mist, and steam. There is much more to designing than this, but it is image more than anything else that takes possession of me and drives me through the design process.

Provincetown Playhouse and
Eugene O'Neill Archival Center,
Provincetown, Massachusetts
Perspective
Charcoal on paper
36 x 40 inches (86 x 102 cm.)

Provincetown Playhouse and
Eugene O'Neill Archival Center,
Provincetown, Massachusetts
Perspective
Charcoal on paper
34 x 40 inches (86 x 102 cm.)

FREDERICK FISHER

Right:
Caplin House, Venice, California
Composite drawing
Ink, pencil, graphite,
and oil pastel on Cranson paper
36 x 27 inches (91 x 67 cm.)

Below:
A subterranean observatory
Section perspective
Ink, pencil, graphite,
and oil pastel on Cranson paper
36 x 27 inches (91 x 67 cm.)

Drawing is one of the iconographic tools used to describe architectural content whether formal, metaphoric, or virtual. Since an icon cannot yield a comprehensive view of the object, these drawings are limited to primary or generating content. Technique is a dependent variable of content. Each of these projects is metaphorically derived.

The observatory is an index for the mechanical relationship between the earth and the cosmos. The drawing concentrates on the geologic texture of the earth and the ambience of the observation chamber.

The Caplin House combines an icon for the owner's youth, which was spent on board a ship (roof as hull), with a social diagram (atrium as communal space). The inverted roof floats on irridescent waves.

The solar crematorium includes a biaxially symmetrical congregation pavilion. Drawn in combination plan, section, and elevation, the formality and symbolic decoration are revealed. Silhouetting the parabolic mirror structure is the sky darkened by an eclipsing sun, implying the project's emotional aspects.

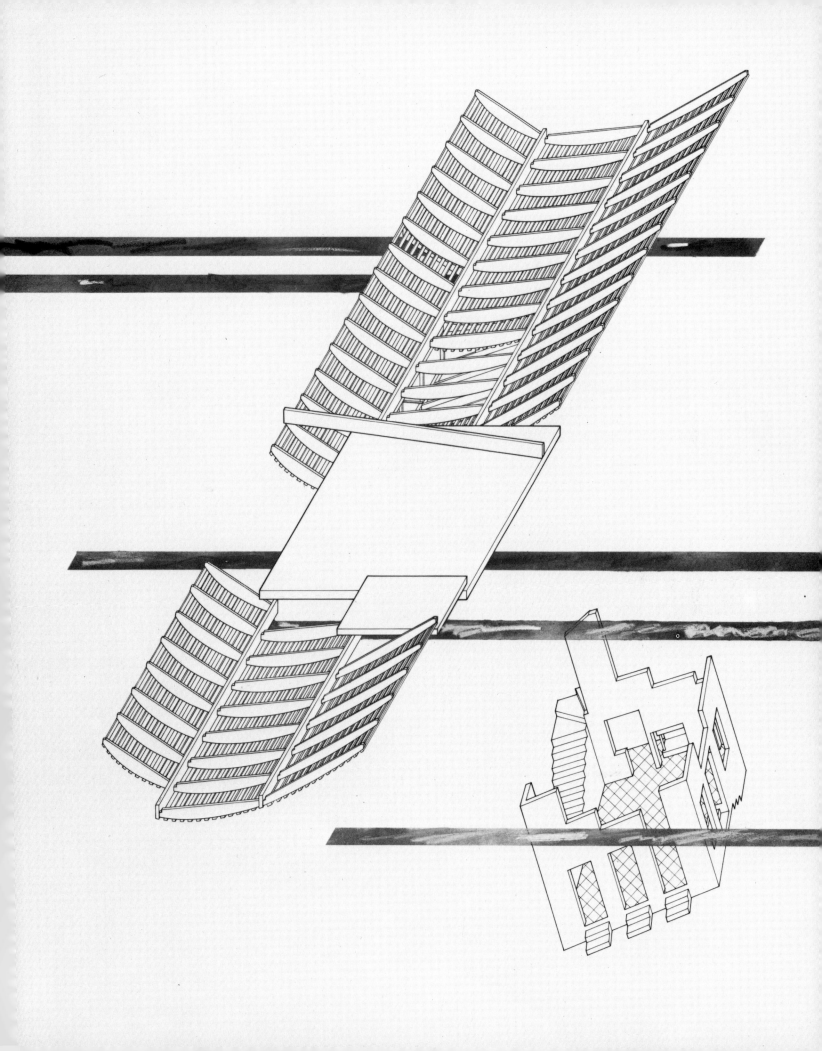

FREDERICK FISHER

A solar crematorium
Composite drawing
Ink, pencil, graphite,
and oil pastel on Cranson paper
36 x 27 inches (91 x 67 cm.)

Jorgensen House, Hollywood, California
Perspective
Ink, graphite, and oil pastel on Cranson paper
36 x 27 inches (91 x 67 cm.)

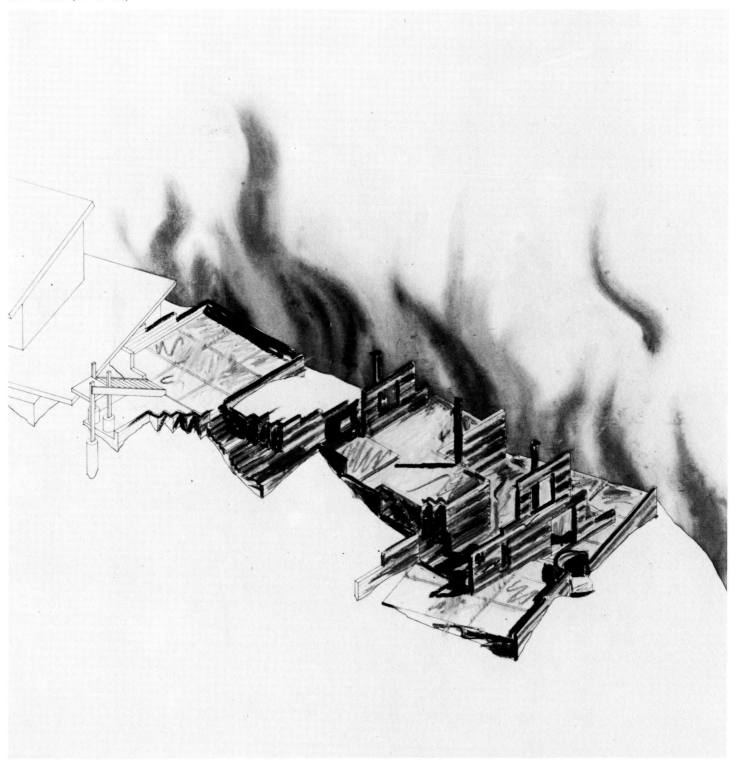

MARK SIMON

Most of these drawings were made not for exhibition but rather as design studies for the renovation of my own house. Although I enjoy drawings and am fond of these, the craft of buildings is my primary interest. Thus I search for favorite shapes and organizing principles through my sketches.

In this project I moved through many ideas and what seemed to be an unending series of sketches drawn at several scales. These were done principally with a very soft pencil on vellum. The pencil is dark and can be seen through several layers of paper, and it is also easily erasable, so both of these facts allowed me a great amount of freedom. I work quickly, changing in a number of different ways what I draw and trying to keep up with the images that come to mind. I also often draw very small to encompass the whole building at once. At times, however, I will draw larger and more complicated images like perspectives in order to sit back and see what I have come up with from a detailed point of view. In this way I move from the inside to the outside of the building, from *parti* to detail, back and forth, back and forth, to find how one affects the other.

Bellamy-Simon House,
Stony Creek, Connecticut
Perspective
Pencil on yellow tracing paper
8½ x 11 inches (22 x 28 cm.)

MARK SIMON

Bellamy-Simon House,
Stony Creek, Connecticut
Perspective
Pencil on yellow tracing paper
8½ x 11 inches (22 x 28 cm.)

Original house and neighbors.

Bellamy-Simon House,
Stony Creek, Connecticut
Elevations
Pencil-lined tracing paper
8½ x 11 inches (22 x 28 cm.)

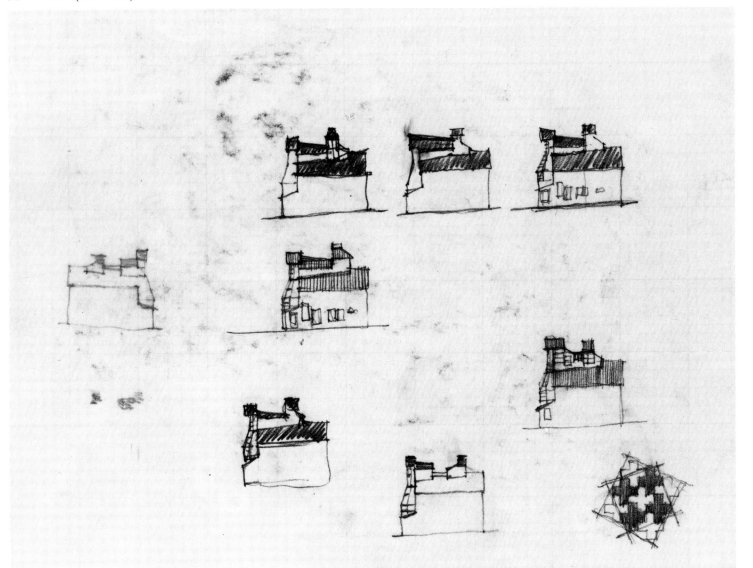

Bellamy-Simon House,
Stony Creek, Connecticut
Elevation
Pencil on yellow tracing paper
8½ x 11 inches (22 x 28 cm.)

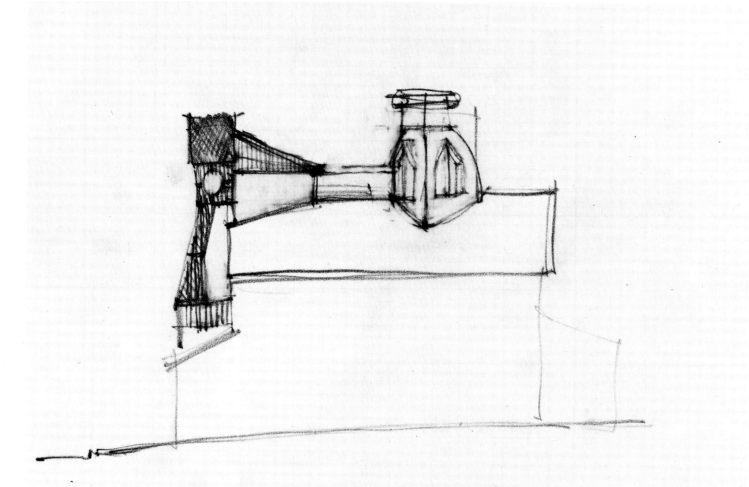

Bellamy-Simon House,
Stony Creek, Connecticut
Elevation
Pencil on yellow tracing paper
8½ x 11 inches (22 x 28 cm.)

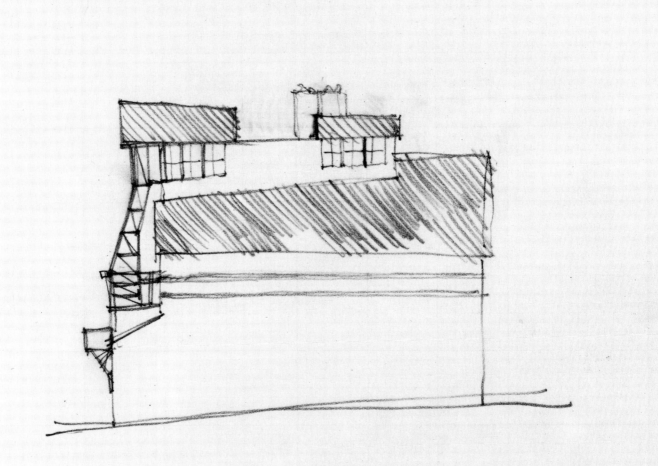

Bellamy-Simon House,
Stony Creek, Connecticut
Plan and section
Pencil on yellow tracing paper
8½ x 11 inches (22 x 28 cm.)

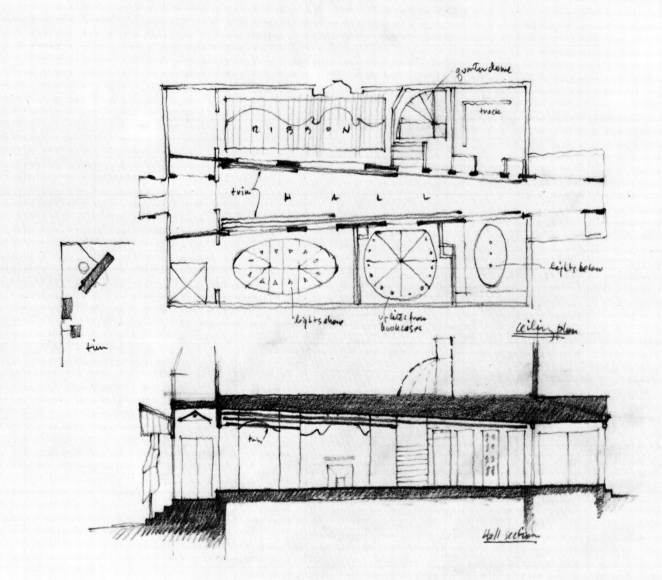

Bellamy-Simon House,
Stony Creek, Connecticut
Plan
Pencil on lined tracing paper
8½ x 11 inches (22 x 28 cm.)

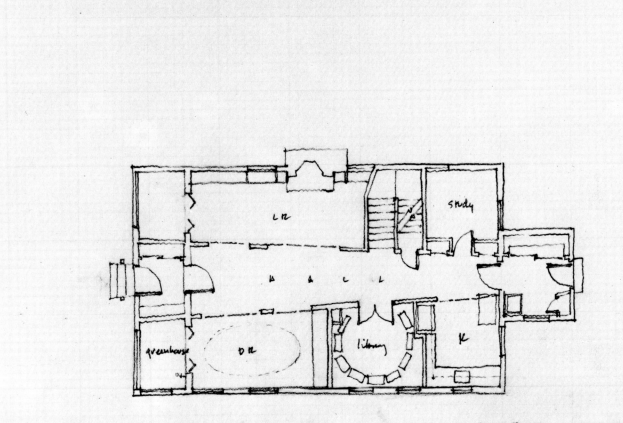

Tile Study, Bellamy-Simon House,
Stony Creek, Connecticut
Plan
Pencil on lined tracing paper
8½ x 11 inches (22 x 28 cm.)

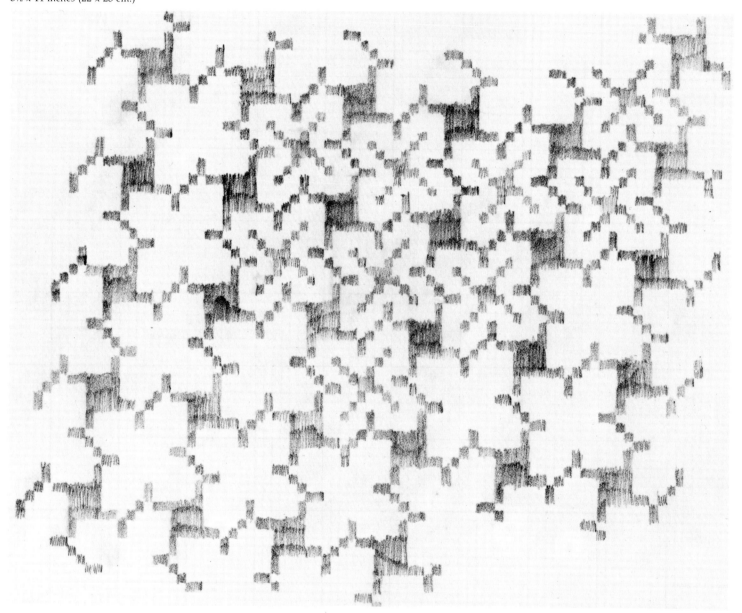

Bellamy-Simon House,
Stony Creek, Connecticut
Elevations
Pencil on yellow tracing paper
8½ x 11 inches (22 x 28 cm.)

Bellamy-Simon House,
Stony Creek, Connecticut
Plan, section, section perspective, and detail
Pencil on lined tracing paper
8½ x 11 inches (22 x 28 cm.)

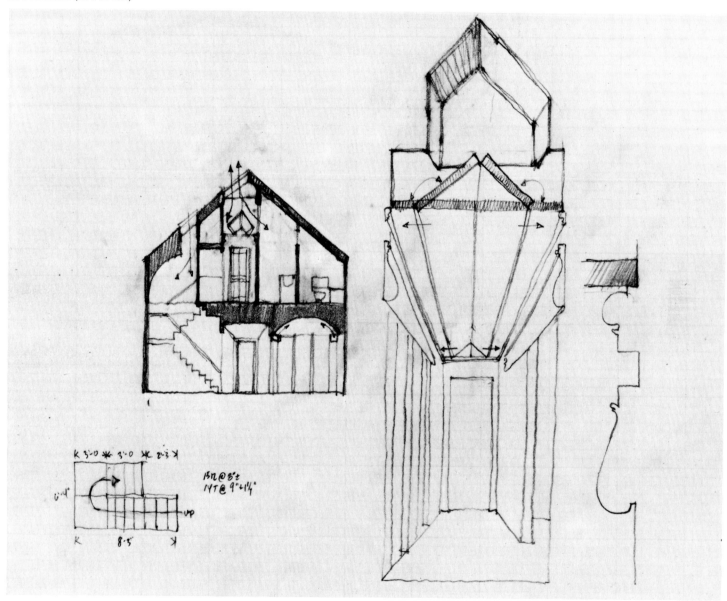

Bellamy-Simon House,
Stony Creek, Connecticut
Elevations and perspective
Pencil on lined tracing paper
8½ x 11 inches (22 x 28 cm.)

JAMES FREED

My work is, as I suspect most work is, in more or less continuous flux, moving from approximate certitude through question to approximate answer and then repeating the cycle.

Having certain ineradicable modernist tendencies that I cherish and nurture, I am inevitably involved with plan, section, and elevation as discipline and with structure as glue. Being concerned with specificity of locale and particularity of use, I am involved with massing, surfaces, and fit. Feeling, more than hearing, the inevitable metaphoric cultural halftones and the mute content of all artifacts, I am involved with bits and pieces of archaic memory, fragments of thought.

I must suppose most architects would, in general, lay claim to all of that. On a very personal level, however, it informs my drawing technique—loose, tentative, questioning, atmospheric, unfinished— which permits me to expose quickly and freely contradictory impulses and emphases and to fashion and read the approximate architectural accommodation. The drawings are in ink in order to discipline the anarchy of formal choice. Intentions mature and develop, but the evolving drawings remain loose—open ended in their particularity—until they are turned into instructional documents.

The desire is that the quick impression of intention remain.

Study for a summer house on a hill
Perspective
Ink on paper
8 x 11 inches (20 x 28 cm.)

Left:
Study for a summer house on a hill
Miscellaneous sketches
Ink on paper
11 x 8 inches (28 x 20 cm.)

Right:
Study for a summer house on a hill
Section
Ink on paper
4 x 6 inches (10 x 15 cm.)

Below:
Study for a summer house on a hill
Perspective
Ink on paper
6 x 8½ inches (15 x 22 cm.)

Study for a summer house on a hill
Perspective
Ink on paper
8 x 11 inches (20 x 28 cm.)

MICHAEL GRAVES

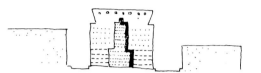

There are three primary categories of architectural drawings, which may be identified according to the architect's intention: the referential sketch, the preparatory study, and the definitive drawing. Several drawings shown here represent the second category of inquiry in that they are preparatory studies for the Portland Public Office Building.

The preparatory study documents the process of inquiry, examining questions raised by a given intention in a manner that provides the basis for later, more definitive work. These drawings are, by nature, deliberately experimental. They produce variations on themes and are clearly exercises toward more concrete architectural ends. Within this general category, however, there is a distinction among the three kinds of drawings: ink sketches assembled from my sketchbooks, serial studies on yellow tracing paper, and a more finished elevation drawing, which served as a color study for the building.

The sketchbook drawings of the elevations, which followed an understanding of the basic plan and overall volume of the building, examined the appropriateness of its character within a general organization of base, middle or body, and top or head.

The yellow tracing paper sketches were developed in series, often overlaid one upon the other. While the series was not wholly linear, the serial approach allowed reexamination and variation of the themes being proposed.

In the third, more finished drawing, where each element is identified to exact scale, I studied the relationship of color to the thematic development and symbolic essence of the work.

Also represented here is an example of my third category, the definitive drawing. This drawing represents the building in three dimensions within the context of the city and the adjacent park.

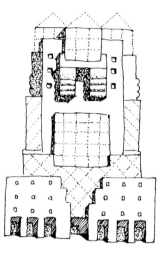

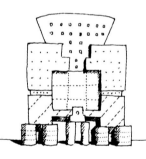

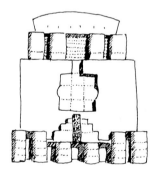

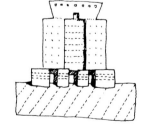

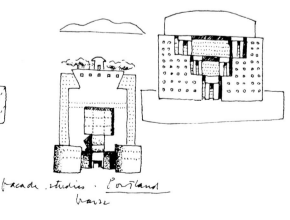

facade studies . Portland
graves

Portland Public Office Building,
Portland, Oregon
Miscellaneous sketches
Ink on paper
12 x 12 inches (30 x 30 cm.)

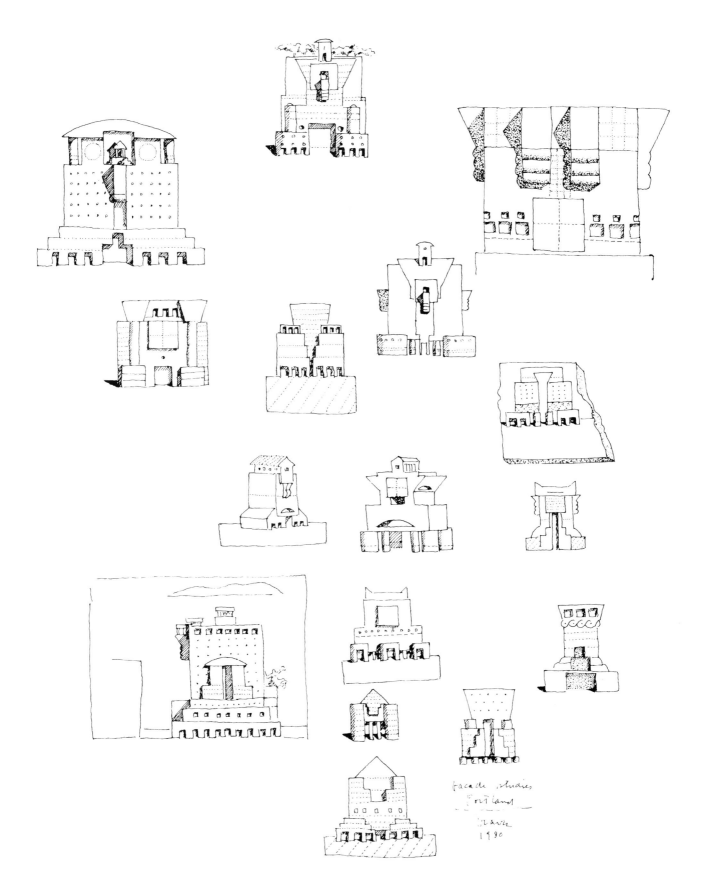

facade studies
Portland

Graves
1980

MICHAEL GRAVES

Fifth Avenue facade,
Portland Public Office Building,
Portland, Oregon
Elevation
Colored pencil on paper
6 x 6 inches (15 x 15 cm.)

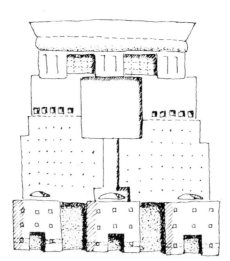

Portland Public Office Building,
Portland, Oregon
Miscellaneous sketches
Ink on paper
12 x 12 inches (30 x 30 cm.)

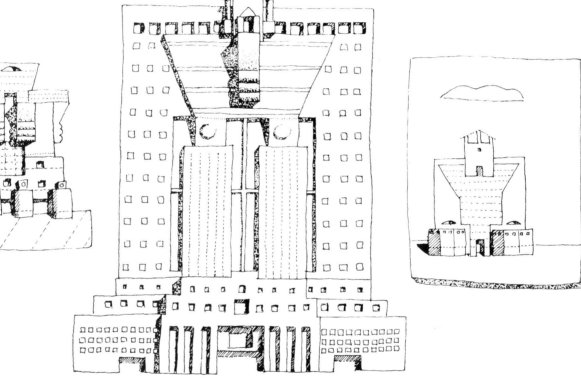

194

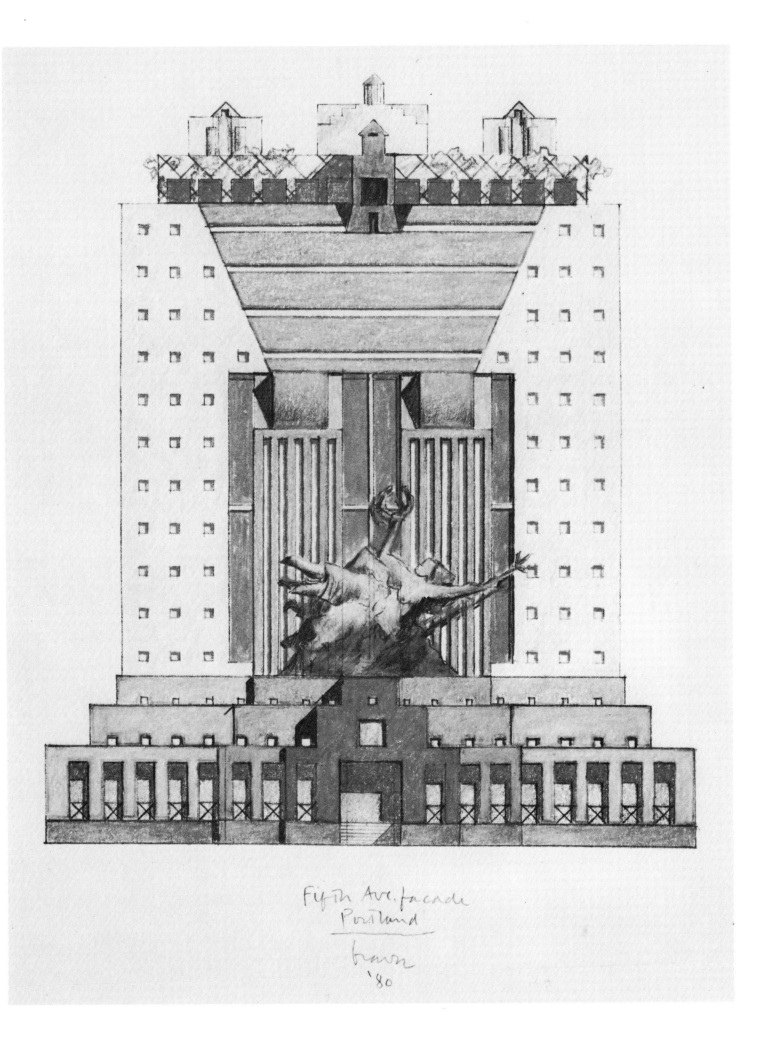

Fifth Ave. facade
Portland

Graves
'80

Portland Public Office Building,
Portland, Oregon
Perspective
Ink on vellum
16½ x 17½ inches (42 x 44 cm.)

BIOGRAPHIES

Gerald Allen was educated at Yale and Cambridge universities and works in New York. He is co-author of *The Place of Houses* and *Dimensions: space, shape & scale in architecture* and author of *Charles Moore: An Architectural Monograph.* He is currently a Visiting Critic at the Graduate School of Design at Harvard.

Thomas Beeby was born in Oak Park, Illinois, and was educated at Yale University. He practices in Chicago in the firm of Hammond, Beeby & Babka and teaches at the University of Illinois, Chicago Circle campus.

Turner Brooks graduated from the Yale School of Architecture in 1970 and practices in Vermont.

F. Andrus Burr was educated at Williams College and the Yale School of Architecture, where he has also taught; he is in practice in New York.

James Coote was educated at Harvard University and teaches at the University of Texas at Austin, where he also practices.

Frederick Fisher was educated at Oberlin College and the University of California at Los Angeles; he practices and teaches in southern California.

James Ingo Freed was born in Germany and educated at the Illinois Institute of Technology; he is a partner in the firm of I.M. Pei & Partners in New York.

Michael Graves was born in Indiana and educated at the University of Cincinnati and at Harvard. He practices in Princeton, New Jersey, and teaches at Princeton University.

Hugh Hardy, Malcolm Holzman, and Norman Pfeiffer are partners in the firm of Hardy Holzman Pfeiffer Associates in New York; they were educated respectively at Princeton University, Pratt Institute, and Columbia University, and all have taught at the Yale School of Architecture.

Helmut Jahn was born in Nuremburg, Germany, has worked with C.F. Murphy Associates since 1967, and has been their Principal and Director of Planning and Design since 1973. In 1981 the firm became Murphy/Jahn.

R.M. Kliment was born in Prague, Czechoslovakia, and graduated from the Yale School of Architecture in 1959; Frances Halsband was born in New York and graduated from the Columbia School of Architecture in 1968. They practice together in New York and have taught at the University of Pennsylvania, Columbia, Yale, and Harvard.

Daniel Libeskind heads the Department of Architecture at the Cranbrook Academy of Art in Michigan. He was born in Poland and educated there, in Israel, at the Cooper Union School of Architecture in New York, and at Essex University in England. He has taught at the University of Kentucky and the University of Toronto and has been a Unit-Master at the Architectural Association in London. His projects have been recently exhibited in Helsinki, London, Zurich, Houston, and New York.

Rodolfo Machado was born in Argentina and studied in Buenos Aires and Paris and at the University of California at Berkeley, where he received an architecture degree in 1970. He is the head of the Department of Architecture at the Rhode Island School of Design. Jorge Silvetti was also born in Argentina and studied there and in the United States. He is an Associate Professor of Architecture at Harvard University. Machado and Silvetti practice architecture together in Boston.

Mark Mack was born in Austria and received a Master of Architecture degree from the Academy of Fine Arts in Vienna. He has worked with the Atelier Hollein in Vienna and with Emilio Ambasz in New York, and he has taught at the University of California at Berkeley.

Henry Meltzer was born in New York and educated at the University of Pennsylvania. He practices in New York, in the field of health care facilities. Richard Oliver was born in California and educated at the University of California at Berkeley, at Cambridge University, and at the University of Pennsylvania. He was formerly Curator of Contemporary Architecture and Design at the Cooper-Hewitt Museum and now practices architecture in New York.

Charles Moore, formerly Dean of the Yale School of Architecture, was educated at the University of Michigan and at Princeton. He now teaches at the University of California in Los Angeles and practices there.

Janet Needham-McCaffrey was educated at the University of Texas at Austin and at the Massachusetts Institute of Technology; she practices urban design in Dallas.

Cesar Pelli was born in Argentina and studied there and at the University of Illinois, where he earned a degree in architecture in 1954. He worked for the next ten years for the office of Eero Saarinen in Michigan and then for Daniel, Mann, Johnson and Mendenhall and for Gruen Associates in Los Angeles. He is now Dean of the Yale School of Architecture and practices in New Haven, Connecticut.

Steven K. Peterson was born in Indiana and educated at Cornell University; he teaches at Columbia University and practices in New York City. Barbara Littenberg was born in New York City and educated at Cornell University; she teaches at Columbia University and practices in New York City.

Stefanos Polyzoides was born in Athens, Greece, in 1946. He received his Bachelor of Arts from Princeton University in 1969 and his Master of Arts in architecture and urban planning from Princeton University in 1972. He taught at Princeton University in 1972–1973 and at the University of Southern California since 1973. His articles have been published in *A + U, Skyline, Casabella, Arquitectura,* and *A.D.* He has written two books, *Schindler's Ephemera* (London, 1981) and *Los Angeles Courtyard Housing* (Los Angeles, 1981). He has practiced architecture since 1973 and is currently with BTA in Los Angeles.

Peter C. Pran was born in Oslo, Norway. He received his Bachelor of Architecture degree from Oslo University and Master of Science in Architecture degree from Illinois Institute of Technology. He is Design Director for Schmidt, Garden & Erikson in Chicago and Adjunct Associate Professor of Architecture at the University of Illinois, Chicago Circle campus.

George Ranalli was born in New York City and educated at the Pratt Institute and Harvard University. He presently teaches at the Yale School of Architecture.

Mark Simon received his architecture degree from the Yale School of Architecture in 1972. He is a partner in the firm of Moore Grover Harper in Essex, Connecticut, and a Visiting Critic at the Yale School of Architecture.

Michael Sorkin was educated at Harvard University and the Massachusetts Institute of Technology; he has taught at the Architectural Association in London and at Columbia University and is also an architectural critic for the *Village Voice* in New York.

Robert A. M. Stern, architect, writer, and teacher, practices in New York and teaches at Columbia University.

Taft Architects was founded in Houston, Texas, in 1972 by John J. Casbarian, Danny Samuels, and Robert H. Timme. They received their undergraduate architectural education at Rice University. John J. Casbarian was born in Alexandria, Egypt, and received a Master of Fine Arts from Cal Arts; he is an Associate Professor at Rice University. Danny Samuels was born in Memphis, Tennessee, and is a Visiting Critic at Rice University. Robert H. Timme was born in Houston and received a Master of Architecture from Rice University; he is an Associate Professor at the University of Houston.

Stanley Tigerman was born in Chicago and educated at the Yale School of Architecture and has taught there. He practices architecture in Chicago.

Robert Venturi was born in Philadelphia and educated at Princeton University. He is the author of *Complexity and Contradiction in Architecture* and co-author with Denise Scott-Brown and Steven Izenour of *Learning from Las Vegas.* **John Rauch** was born in Philadelphia and educated at the University of Pennsylvania. **Denise Scott-Brown** was born in Zambia and educated at the Architectural Association in London and at Princeton University. They practice together in Philadelphia.

Lauretta Vinciarelli received a doctoral degree in architecture and urban planning from the University of Rome in 1971 and was formerly a member of the faculty at the Pratt Institute in New York. She is an Assistant Professor at Columbia University and practices in New York and Texas.

Bartholomew Voorsanger was educated at Princeton and Harvard; **Edward Mills** was educated at North Carolina State University and Harvard. Together they practice architecture in New York in the firm of Voorsanger & Mills.

Edited by Sharon Lee Ryder, Stephen A. Kliment, and Susan Davis
Designed by Robert Fillie
Graphic production by Ellen Greene
Set in 12 point Palatino